A practic intriguing
experimenus unav ... lves.

*By the same author*
ASTRAL DOORWAYS
MINDREACH
REINCARNATION: FIVE KEYS TO PAST LIVES

# EXPERIMENTAL MAGIC

*by*

J. H. BRENNAN

*Illustrations by*

*Helen Brennan and Brendan P. Carey*

THE AQUARIAN PRESS
Wellingborough, Northamptonshire

First published 1972
This edition first published 1984



British Library Cataloguing in Publication Data

Brennan, J. H.
Experimental magic.
1. Magic
I. Title
133.4'3 BF 1611

ISBN 0-85030-423-7

Printed in Great Britain by
Richard Clay (The Chaucer Press) Ltd,
Bungay, Suffolk

CONTENTS

# INTRODUCTION

Over the years, I have read many hundreds of books on magic and the occult. I cannot now remember one that did not leave me with a faint sense of something missing.

Eventually I decided that the something missing was commitment. Few authors have been rash enough to stress a personal belief that magic works. Fewer still have had the guts to spell out in simple language what exactly happens when you embark on a magical experiment. In this book I have tried to avoid both errors. In the attempt I may have gained some insight into why they occur so frequently.

First, claiming magic works in the age of the computer makes you feel a fool. It goes against the grain, against everything you have been taught, against everything that is real and practical and worthwhile around you. So, feeling a fool, you say that magic works and keep wondering if you have not been hallucinating or taken in by coincidence. And since you have also decided to spell out in simple terms what happens, you are deprived of that great cloak worn by most magicians – the aura of dark mystery.

Once you put it into practice, magic is not nearly so dramatic, not anywhere nearly so glamorous as it might have once appeared. Much of it is hard slog and repetition. Results appear without theatricals. This can be disappointing, but at least it is a lot less disappointing than trying something out with no results at all.

I have tried to keep theory to a minimum. But it is not possible to ignore it altogether. Bear with me in speculative chapters: it is nice to know what you are doing as well as how to do it. This is not to say that even the minimum of theory in this book should be accepted as dogma. The only roads to truth I know are experience and meditation. Meditate on the theories and draw your own conclusions. Try the experiments and learn by your mistakes.

One thing you are going to discover very quickly is that suggestion and auto-suggestion play a large part in magical working. I mention this lest you feel tempted to dismiss the entire system for this reason. Before you do, try duplicating magical effects by suggestion alone. You will find you can't.

Another discovery you will make quickly is that much magical technique is concerned with manipulating the imagination. Here again, temptations to dismiss the system out of hand arise. I can only express my personal belief that imagination is perhaps the most underrated function of the human mind; and suggest you withhold judgement until you try it.

One final word. You may notice a certain light-hearted, even frivolous, approach in certain chapters, particularly those dealing with Low Magic. It is there for two reasons. The first is that I am tired of the woodenly portentious style affected by most authors on the subject, and I fancy you may be too. The second is simply that Low Magic can be fun.

It will remain fun – and High Magic will remain safe – just so long as you take care to remember you are working with a very potent system.

# PART ONE – LOW MAGIC

## CHAPTER ONE

## CONTACTING SPIRITS

Magic works. But failure rate is high and success (sometimes) a terrifying experience. The systems – for there are more than one – require careful study and quite monumental effort. Only the individual can judge whether the effort is worthwhile, although occasionally rewards come from unexpected directions.

It is, for instance, possible to produce a five-pound note by magic. The system which will do the trick requires a minimum of four months' daily study and one month's daily application. A charlady could produce the same amount in less than a week by the simple expedient of sweeping floors.

But where the magician differs from the charlady is in the side benefits he obtains. His willpower and powers of concentration are strenuously exercised. His ability to visualize is improved. His understanding of the universe becomes a little deeper, as does his understanding of himself. And it is likely that his five-pound note will give him more satisfaction than the charlady could ever feel.

Magicians are curious people and magic a curious subject. It embraces, at one end of the spectrum, blatant charlatanism and, at the other, the fascinating realm of depth psychology. It is broad enough to take in table-tapping, divination, hypnotism and the Catholic Mass. It is powerful enough to bring you face to face with God . . . or plunge you into lunacy.

At the root of magic lies the First Law: 'Know Thyself'.

When a doctor writes on medicine, or a psychiatrist on the human mind, it is usual to present credentials so that the reader may judge the real weight of the author's words. Regrettably, there is no equivalent of the M.D. in magic. Certain groups donate high-sounding titles, but, without a standard of comparison, their worth is difficult to ascertain. Like the artist or the poet, the magician must be judged partially on what he does and partially on what he is. No one is a better judge of either than himself.

My first textbook of magic was Blavatsky's *The Secret Doctrine*, six volumes which I still find virtually impossible to understand. My first experiments were little better than a parlour game. But I was young and they had fascination and they led to better things.

I propose to give an outline of some of those 'better things' in subsequent pages, along with an outline of initial experiments, childish though they may seem.

And, as I did in my first book, I propose to give a warning. The warning is simply that, like electricity, magic can be dangerous unless treated with respect. How seriously you view this warning is a matter for yourself.

In the days before Belfast was set alight by petrol bombs, I travelled to an old Victorian house off University Road to court Helen and discuss the Summerland with her landlady, Miss Johanna Kerr.

Helen found Johanna fascinating and, when I met her, so did I. She was a very pale, very blonde, faintly neurotic spinster, approaching forty with a distinct feeling of unease. She was the first medium I had ever met, a natural psychic improved by Spiritualist training, who specialized in healing.

She entertained us to tea in a cold drawing-room heavy with archaic furniture and, once satisfied that our interest was more than frivolous, agreed to contact spirits with an inverted whisky glass.

The unique appeal of this little magical operation lies in the fact that it needs neither preparation, training, nor elaborate equipment. What it does need is a glass, a polished table-top, the letters of the alphabet and a minimum of three people.

Probably the trickiest item is the alphabet. Lexicon cards are ideal, but if you don't happen to have any handy, the simplest way is to write the letters on squares of paper. It is a good idea to add 'Yes' and 'No' squares as well. The figures 1 to 10 can also be helpful.

Arrange the letters in order in a circle round the table. Leave reasonable space between each one. If you are using 'Yes' and 'No' squares, place them in an East/West position. Next invert the glass in the centre of the table. Almost any type of glass will do, so long as it moves freely over the polished surface and does not have a stem.

At the start of the seance, each one present sits in a circle round the table and places one finger of either hand lightly on the bottom of the glass, preferably at the edge. After that, the only further ingredient needed is patience.

On our first attempt, it took twenty minutes before the glass began to move. But move it did. Johanna, who was too accustomed to these things to feel embarrassment, asked the traditional question, 'Is anybody there?' The glass shuddered slightly, then, with growing speed, began to circle the letters. Eventually it returned to the centre and waited.

We asked our questions, many of them asinine to a degree, and the glass spelt out its answers. Afterwards, Johanna confessed she never felt entirely happy about glass-moving. Such physical phenomena tended to block out the spiritual truths of her religion.

Since that evening, I have used this crude form of ouija more times than I can count. Today I don't feel entirely happy about it either, although for different reasons from those which troubled Johanna.

The first question to be asked is why the glass moves. And the first answer is the obvious one: Because it's pushed. Obvious or not, the objection is virtually impossible to overcome. A joker, providing he acts with subtlety, simply cannot be detected. The only real safeguard is to know your friends and make sure they are willing to engage in the experiment without prejudice.

Assuming any conscious fraud is absent, the possibility of unconscious influence arises. For years I was convinced this must be the explanation. (I was then reluctant to accept the possibility of spirit intervention.) But a psychiatrist disabused me.

'How many people attend these seances?'

'Five or six.'

'Then you would have five or six unconscious minds influencing the direction of the glass. The result would be garble. But it wasn't garble, was it?'

It was not.

Unfortunately it does not tend to be a particularly inspiring communication either. Whatever the psychiatrists may say about unconscious minds, my own experience has been that the glass reacts to the mood of the gathering.

I have watched glass-moving played as a party game – under the curious name of 'Hookie' – and it produced light-hearted party answers. A less light-hearted experiment, conducted by devotees of Dennis Wheatley, actually contacted Satan, with vaguely comic opera results.

Between these extremes are a hundred and one variations. And among the variations are a few surprises. Regular sitters will tend to find that as their series of experiments progresses, there is much less variation in the type of 'contact' made. A single entity will come through again and again until, as often happens, a very clear personality picture of the 'spirit' is built up. Most of the surprises will arise from the abilities shown by the entity.

It is best to admit the truth and the truth is that the greater percentage of communications received by means of glass-moving is rubbish. This holds good even when experiments are undertaken with commendable seriousness of purpose. But the exceptions are worth searching out. A few drawn from personal experience may be of interest.

We were seated round Johanna's heavy polished table, determined to discover if our glass-moving spirit could predict the future. Paul, who suggested the experiment, was careful to sit distant from us in another corner of the room. He wanted to make sure he did not influence the glass unconsciously. All he proposed to do was ask questions and take notes.

'Will I change my job?' asked Paul.

'Yes,' spelt out the glass.

'What will I do?'

'Study.'

'What will I study?'

'Art.'

'Where will I study art?'

'London.'

Every answer in this short sequence proved to be totally

inaccurate. Paul failed to change his job and never became an art student in London or anywhere else. Yet the experiment was not a complete failure. Prior to the experiment, Paul had concealed some facts from us. The facts were these: Paul had become, in recent months, dissatisfied with his job and determined to make a change. He concluded his real future lay as a painter and, with a view to equipping himself for such a career, had decided to study art. For personal reasons he preferred not to enter the Belfast College of Art and had applied for a scholarship which would take him to London.

If this is a coincidence, it is rather a long one. Apart from myself, none of the sitters knew him prior to the experiment; and he had carefully kept his plans from me.

Telepathy seems a much more reasonable theory. It is supported by the fact that Helen reports she used the glass very successfully in the past for telepathic experiments between her brother and herself.

Occasionally the glass will bring gratuitous information. In the middle of an evening's seance, the glass suddenly spelt out, 'Contact Sheila.'

'Who is the message for?' I asked.

'You.'

'Why should I contact Sheila?'

'She needs help.'

'Why does she need help?'

'She is ill.'

I had not seen Sheila for some months. But at least I had no qualms about getting in touch now. She was a psychic and a witch, perfectly prepared to accept that people should act on occult communications. I rang her home, but there was no reply.

By the third day of phone calls with the same negative result, I was growing distinctly uneasy. Although Sheila's husband did not altogether share Sheila's views about the unknown, I decided to risk phoning him at work. He was not there. He and Sheila had gone off on holiday. I concluded that nobody goes off on holiday if they are feeling ill, marked the communication down as inaccurate and forgot the whole thing.

Weeks later I met Sheila by accident and told her the story. Then she told me she had at the time gone on holiday to prepare herself for a very serious operation. At the time of our glass-moving, she had indeed been ill.

This instance, and the one previously quoted, illustrate the strangeness of certain glass-moving effects. But despite this strangeness, in neither case was there any importance to be attached to the message. It did not matter that Paul was thinking of moving to London to study art, for he did not go. It did not matter that I failed to reach Sheila, for what she needed (and found) was a competent surgeon.

Over the years I have seen other examples of this strangeness. A man told by the glass he had been a sailor in a previous incarnation was later shown to have a periodic emotional obsession about going to sea. Another, who asked for a reply in Spanish, got it without garble, despite the fact that none of the sitters spoke the language. Then, just as one's belief in spirit entities is strengthening, someone suggests blindfolding the sitters. We agree, and garble results.

It may be disconcerting to find so much space devoted to a parlour game in a book on experimental magic. But the approach has purpose.

First, almost anyone can undertake the game. And once you do, it will soon become apparent that you get out no more than you put in. Try it once or twice in a frivolous frame of mind and you will have a pleasant evening's entertainment, no more. Try it seriously and the answers will be serious, although generally unimportant.

But to reach the strangeness takes time, as if glass-moving generates strangenesses as slowly as an oyster generates a pearl. If you can bear to wait and persevere, this little operation may become worthwhile. Not for the strangenesses themselves, which are often little more than a bizarre talking-point, but for the lesson in patience.

Every magical operation requires patience. Major ones require most patience of all. Preparations can go on for days, months, or even years. And like a laboratory experiment, the final result, even then, may be failure. It requires a resilient personality to accept this and try again.

Glass-moving, childish though it may be, teaches another important lesson besides patience – the lesson of discrimination. It is a vital lesson for anyone wishing to investigate magic.

The magical edifice has a glitter which fascinates the mind and can quickly overcome it altogether. Any unprejudiced reading of the Medieval grimoires, for instance, will reveal a depth of pathology that is truly staggering. Yet even today those grimoires can still claim their lunatic adherents.

Far less dramatic, but just as dangerous in its own way, is the fast slide into superstition which claims some beginners in these Arts. Lives are lived in desperate fear of omens, or frantic calculations of the favourable days and times. Such nonsense might be laughable, if it were not such a serious business when it gets a grip of the imagination.

So far as I know, the only real defence against this type of obsession is discrimination; and glass-moving, with its high percentage of silly messages teaches discrimination as no other method can. The process is so lacking in real glamour that the risk of self-deception is virtually cancelled out.

And on top of everything else, there is still the lively mental exercise to be found in the basic mystery of why the glass moves at all. Fraud or trickery? Unconscious pushing? Spirit intervention? Psychokinesis or telepathy? Or perhaps a combination of these elements.

Only personal experience will bring your answer. My own, still far from certain, is based on the occult doctrine of the Artificial Elemental. But that is something for discussion in a later chapter.

## CHAPTER TWO

# WHY MAGIC WORKS

When you learn arithmetic or algebra, certain facts are held to be self-evident. Two plus two will always equal four, no matter what the circumstances. If $a = b$ and $b = c$, then $a = c$.

Magic too is based on a vital axiom. Every magical cause works from the inside out; and there are no such things as miracles.

The common man's idea of magic is conditioned by the fairy tale. He expects a thunderclap to follow the waving of a wand. And a shower of gold to follow up the thunderclap. Even the most sophisticated are a little disappointed when nothing of this sort is produced by a magical operation. Tell a friend you are studying magic and he will ask you for a conjuring trick without the mirrors. No wonder certain of the Lodges add discretion to discrimination as prime virtues for the trainee.

Dion Fortune describes magic as 'The art of producing changes of consciousness at will' and by doing so tells only half the story. Effects follow magical changes of consciousness. But they follow in their own good time, through natural channels.

To understand all this requires a grasp of magical theory, which is not the easiest thing in the world even when the theory is presented in its simplest form.

Virtually everyone (except scientists and a few lunatic philosophers like ourselves) subscribes to the idea that Mind and Matter are two different things. This appears self-evident and so is seldom questioned. Sometimes these aspects of our life are looked upon as direct opposites, like black and white, sometimes as complementaries, like yin and yang. But opposite or complementary, they are different – that is the important thing.

And that is the one thing the magician denies.

To the magician, mind and matter are a continuity. At one level he will agree with the Vedic Sages that the world is an illusion. At another, he will simply assume certain mental gymnastics can produce certain physical effects, because ultimately there is no difference between the two.

How the magician arrives at this extraordinary conclusion is neither here nor there. He may indeed accept it merely as an article of faith, a working hypothesis which allows him to get on with the job. There might even be a cause to make for the proposition that the conclusion is untrue, that magic works for some other reason altogether. Such a case will not worry the magician. His methods are interesting, his results reasonable. Despite the cynics, life is good.

Let us assume you are still agog at my throwaway reference in Chapter One to the magical production of a five-pound note. The example is admittedly mundane, but not nearly so frivolous as it may appear at first. Most of us devote a great proportion of our time and energy in continuing attempts to produce five-pound notes with a greater or lesser degree of success. A description of a magical effort towards the same end will illustrate vividly the differences in approach and basic thinking.

If you analyse the normal ways of getting the five-pound note, you will find they break down into four distinct sequence headings – Desire, Belief, Action and Reaction.

First comes the desire for the money. If that is lacking, obviously you will take no steps to get it.

Next comes belief in your ability to earn five pounds. Again this is a vital step of the process. Without it, you will freeze into helplessness.

Next comes action. You may decide to buy a coat and sell it at a profit. You might set a five-pound fee on some service that is within your capabilities.

And finally reaction. The coat is sold, the service accepted. The result is you receive five pounds.

In this sequence, almost all the emphasis is placed on the action. The remaining factors obviously must be present, but they operate almost at a reflex level and no one pays a great deal of attention to them.

A magician follows the same sequence, but the placing of the emphasis is vastly different.

An old word of advice goes, 'Inflame thyself with Prayer.' Desire must be stoked to white heat. It is desire which provides the fuel for the operation; and the higher the octane, the better the results. It is no mean feat to maintain a single burning desire for days and weeks on end, but the magician, to have best chance of success, must achieve it. This single factor, more than any other, is the reason why few advanced magicians bother with such trivia as five-pound notes. There are bigger fish to catch in so strong a net.

Belief too is just as important to the magician. A feeble take-it-for-granted self-confidence is not enough. He strains for inner certainty, the utter conviction that he cannot fail. And this is the factor which tempts beginners to base their experiments towards results which do not matter. In theory there is no real magical difference between producing £5 or £50,000, but few beginners have the necessary conviction to achieve the latter figure.

By contrast, the action taken has much less emphasis. It is mere routine, and an inward one at that. And when the routine is finished, the magician waits. He knows results are seldom quick, and never miraculous. The five-pound note will come eventually. And so it does. It may arrive by post, the return of a long-forgotten loan. It may arrive by hand, a spontaneous gift from an admirer. But arrive it will . . . through perfectly natural channels.

What is this curious routine the magician follows to conjure up his five-pound note? Oddly enough, it varies. And still more oddly, the variation does not seem to matter.

We have it on the authority of Frazer that the primitive shaman accepts certain correspondences in the universe. He has grown up with this belief, so that the correspondences are as natural to him as his walk. He has no sophistication and his system is primitive, based on the nonsense equation 'Like = Like'.

Water sprinkled from a pan is like the falling of rain. So to produce rain it is necessary to sprinkle water from a pan. Whistling imitates the sound of the wind. So it is possible to whistle up a storm. This is sympathetic magic and its roots run deep. How many men are convinced they have only to wash the car to bring on a downpour? Sailors discourage whistling on board ship. It is considered unlucky, a storm-bringer.

Nowadays, in the West at any rate, no one believes in sympathetic magic. It is altogether too crude to be possible. Without belief, the four-step sequence falls apart. The high grade occultist finds himself unable to perform an operation which would give no trouble to his simple-minded brother in the bush. But it does not matter. Magic has not died, merely increased in complexity.

Today's student of the Arts is taught a new set of correspondences. What they are depends largely on his school. Probably the most widespread are drawn from the Hebrew Qabalah, with additional material courtesy of Aleister Crowley. The Qabalah is well looked on, as befits a great mystical system. Crowley is not. But even his most strenuous opponents are not averse to making use of his work, just as today many Britishers delight in driving a car originally planned by Hitler.

If the magician has been trained in this system, he will, before his actual experiment, have built into his mind a series of associations with hard cash. He will, for instance, associate it with a planet and a colour and a particular sphere of the Tree of Life. At the simplest level of working, he will flood his aura with the associated colour (by an act of imagination) and visualize strongly the five-pound note coming to him. If he wishes to go further, he may surround himself with further associations. He may even perform ritual actions of symbolic value. All have exactly the same purpose – to turn his mind in the right direction and keep it there.

The basic chain of associations is as follows.

| | |
|---|---|
| Sephirah: | Tiphareth |
| Colour: | Gold |
| Planet: | The Sun |

All this seems too easy to be true. But simply knowing the links will not necessarily attach the chain to anything. The magician is a worker if nothing else. He will spend weeks, months, perhaps even years in daily meditation on the spheres of the Tree of Life, building their associations into the deepest levels of his being, making them a part of him, slowly realizing why the associations hold good and what they mean. Only after that will he feel truly confident about his fiver. And by that time, as you will see, he may have bigger fish to fry than five-pound notes.

How does it work, this fascinating conjuration of a five-pound note? Many magicians have not the slightest idea. They learned the method (as you can in later pages), did their preparatory homework and found, eventually, the cash came home to roost. The power of magic was proved by the experiment.

But magic is not a power. It is a system or a collection of systems. When a television set works, it does not prove there is a power of electronics. It merely demonstrates the practical application of certain principles. These principles may be a mystery even to the man who repairs the set. All he needs to know is which wire joins on to what. And the same may well go for the man who manufactures it.

It is probably true to say that the most penetrating insight into why the five-pound note trick works did not come from a magician. It came instead from that wily old psychologist, Carl Gustav Jung. Unfortunately, Jung's literary style is not a patch on Freud's, with the result that many of his best ideas lie buried underneath a mass of academic verbiage.

Like most clinical psychiatrists, Jung came across some very odd occurrences while treating patients. Unlike most, he chose not to ignore them. From this simple difference was born the theory of synchronicity. An actual case history will make the theory clear.

Jung, at one stage of his career, was treating a patient, Mr X, for an emotional disorder. Apart from this disorder, Mr X seemed fit and well.

Then, after one treatment session, Mr X complained of a sore throat. This is not the sort of symptom which disturbs a layman, but Jung's medical experience led him to suspect there might be more behind it than a cold in the chest. He felt there was an outside possibility of heart disease and advised the man to see his doctor. Mr X agreed. En route to the surgery (and unknown to Jung at the time) he collapsed from a heart attack and died.

Meanwhile Mrs X entered the story. She called Jung in something of a panic to ask if there was anything seriously wrong with her husband.

Pause now to consider, as Jung must have done. Mr X was being treated for a *psychiatric* illness. Such ailments, although uncomfortable, are rarely fatal. Although Mrs X may well have known about her husband's sore throat, she was unlikely to have made the same diagnosis as Jung did. Indeed, at that time, Jung himself did not know his guess had been proved dramatically correct.

He reassured her within the limitations of the circumstances and asked her what had prompted the question. Her answer was curious: a flock of birds had arrived at her husband's bedroom window.

To make sense of this answer requires knowledge of Mrs X's background. Years before, as her grandfather lay dying, a flock of birds came to his bedroom window. The same thing occurred on the death of her father. Because of this, Mrs X had learned to associate the arrival of birds with death. The flock at the window became a personal omen.

When the omen proved correct three times running, Jung began to ponder the mechanics of its operation. He began with two contentions, both of which are logically beyond question.

1. Flocks of birds arriving at windows do not cause death. If they did, half the human race would have been wiped out long ago.

2. Human death does not attract birds. Otherwise our hospitals would be faced with a gigantic problem.

In short, no cause-and-effect relationship exists between the birds and the death. But that does not mean no relationship exists at all. Self-evidently *something* was going on; and it was plain enough to prompt Mrs X to call Jung.

Jung concluded a relationship did indeed exist. But it was a relationship outside the usual cause-and-effect sequence. He felt a second sequence was at work in the world, largely hidden from immediate attention. The link between the two factors in the case was Meaning. Meaning is a function of the human mind. The link between Mr X's death and the flock of birds at his bedroom window then became, almost incredibly, the mind (and/or belief) of Mrs X. Jung considered he had discovered an acausal connecting principle and he labelled it 'meaningful coincidence' or 'synchronicity'.

Synchronicity is a fairy-tale conclusion, an open invitation to the idea that wishing will make it so. Even coming from Jung it might have remained no more than a theory if he had not set out to test his conclusions by experiment.

Jung's manner of experiment was both bizarre and delightful. He looked around for a suitable tool to test synchronicity and found it in the ancient pseudo-science of astrology. Astrologers accept that certain planetary configurations give clues to the likelihood of situations and occurrences. Belief in astrological relationships goes back for centuries, possibly millenia. Yet the actions of men cannot influence the planets in their courses; and, if some mysterious planetary rays influenced the actions of men, astrology would be an exact science, which even its supporters admit it is not.

With this tool, the stage was set for an experiment. Jung searched the horoscopes of selected married couples for the traditional marriage conjunctions. He found a percentage of cases in which the conjunctions did indeed occur. Then he analysed his findings statistically and found the percentage was significantly above chance expectation.

Astrologers rejoiced that a respected psychiatrist had proved the truth of astrology. In fact, he had done nothing of the sort: rather he had proved there was a certain truth *in* astrology. But he concluded, with reason, that he had proved the truth of his synchronicity theory.

The discovery of an acausal connection principle in nature was as shattering in its own way as Einstein's $E = mc^2$. But since its practical application was less evident than the A-bomb, synchronicity has been largely ignored. Only the lunatic fringe, of which the magicians find themselves uncomfortable members, pay attention to the weirdness Jung discovered. And since no one believes in magic anyway, their claims have been met with knowing smiles.

There is, I feel, a case to be made for changing the name

'magician'. 'Synchronisicist' is more impressive, up-to-date and, consequently, more acceptable. Although it won't change the fact that synchronisicists work magic.

CHAPTER THREE

# OCCULT ANATOMY

Occult anatomy is not an easy subject. But you will need to grasp its rudiments before you can successfully undertake the five-pound note trick . . . or other, more important, operations.

The Magus is at one with the Mystic, who teaches we are at One with the All. What this means, in rather more banal terms, is that you are part of the universe and subject to its laws. Because of this, everything that happens in the universe influences you, if only to an infinitesimal degree. And, conversely, everything you do reacts (to the same minute degree) on the entire universe.

This disturbing thought is probably easy enough to accept on the physical level, but there are, of course, other levels to consider. In order to keep the picture as simple as possible, I shall limit the discussion to two further levels only – the mental and the spiritual.

The magician believes that these three levels, forming part of a super-embracing All, grade into one another and have certain distinct points of contact. Further, on the evidence of mystics and clairvoyants, he feels he has a fair idea of what the inner levels are like.

He sees himself surrounded, as it were, by a vast, inexhaustible sea of spiritual energy. The extent of the power available is literally beyond imagination. But at least part of the power is fortunately not beyond control. The problems are really contact and transformation. Your light won't work until wires make contact with the power source; and since few of your household gadgets will work on direct current, a transformer is needed somewhere along the line.

Contact with the spiritual power source should, in theory, be an easy, natural thing. You are part of the One, so this aspect of the One should flow through you without hindrance. But it is hindered, quite unconsciously, by one of mankind's most prevalent habits – tension.

Tension is much more insidious than most people imagine. I have watched patients maintain from the edge of their seats that they were perfectly relaxed. Tension creeps in undetected and establishes itself as a habit pattern. Sometimes the habit is a tricky one to break. But break it will, with time and practice.

This is how to break the tension habit.

Leave aside a time each day to practise relaxation. Ten or fifteen minutes is enough in the early stages; although you can increase this later if you like. Early morning is the best time: there are less distractions and far fewer temptations to do something else.

Next, get firmly into your mind that you are going to practise relaxation *every day*. It is, in fact, worth doing every day for the rest of your life, much more worthwhile than your present daily ritual of cleaning your teeth and combing your hair. And the continuing sequence is important. Even two minutes daily practice is worth several hours at irregular intervals.

With this in mind, you are ready to begin. Make your first attempts on your bed, lying flat on your back with your hands by your sides. Your unconscious mind, which has a lot to do with habit formation, associates bed with sleep and hence relaxation: so by performing your first exercises on a bed, you are automatically taking a step towards the desired result.

In theory, relaxation is the easiest thing in the world, simply a matter of 'letting go'. In actuality, it is usually a learned response nowadays, built up by conscious practice and much repetition.

In order to be sure of complete relaxation, it is first necessary to be aware of tension. This may sound very obvious, but the fact remains that very few people are genuinely aware of tension in a particular set of muscles. At best (or worst) they experience the general effect in terms of discomfort.

So your first job is to stimulate awareness. Begin with your feet. Curl the toes downwards and inwards, as if you were trying to pick up a handkerchief. When you have done so, hold that position . . . and keep holding it until the toes are uncomfortable to the point of cramping. This discomfort will make you fully aware of the deliberate tension in the toe muscles. Once you are fully aware, let go.

Now go further. Bend your feet forward and hold them so until the discomfort occurs. Then let go.

Now move on to the calf muscles, tensing them to the point of discomfort . . . then letting go.

Continue with the sequence, moving slowly and deliberately up your body. Take your time so that no set of muscles open to conscious influence is left out. When you reach your face, grit your teeth and grimace. Then let go.

Finally, remember that the scalp has muscles too. Frown to bring the scalp forward, hold it . . . then let go.

By the time you have finished the sequence, it is likely enough that some tension will have crept back into the muscles you treated earlier, so do a mental roll-call and if tension is discovered anywhere, increase it to the point of conscious discomfort . . . then let go.

Now put the whole lot together. Strain every tendon and fibre of your body. Then let go . . . and relax. If you have been accustomed to tension, you will find the experience of complete conscious relaxation a very pleasant one. Practise it daily.

After you have got the hang of the conscious relaxation sequence, after, that is, you can do it easily and fluently as a matter of routine, the time has come to improve the level of your performance. In doing so, you will learn a trick which will be of very considerable benefit to you in everyday life.

At this stage it is wise to dispense with the bed. Continue your morning exercises in a chair. There is a good reason for this. As your depth of relaxation increases, so does the danger of falling asleep. Since you have better things to do, this should be avoided. If you practise relaxation in a chair and fall asleep, you will also fall off. It is a rude awakening, but a sure one.

Make yourself comfortable in your chair. You are about to add a breathing exercise to the basic relaxation.

Breathing exercises, particularly those of the Yoga system, can cause Westerners a lot of trouble. Even the one given here, simple though it is, should not be overdone, especially in the early stages. Do not use it for more than three minutes on your first attempt and build it up slowly, minute by minute, over a period of weeks. Should any trouble arise, stop the exercise immediately.

Avoid also breathing too deeply in the early stages. Here again, depth of breathing should be built up very gradually over the weeks.

One final word of warning. This exercise involves retaining breath. This should be done by holding out the abdominal muscles, *not* by closing the throat. And if you feel any strain whatever during the exercise, you are doing it wrong.

Now the exercise itself. First, empty your lungs. There is no need to empty them completely in the early stages and certainly no need to force.

Now breathe in to the mental count of four. If you find you have taken a full breath before finishing the count, regulate your speed of counting. Do not attempt to force more air in. The object of this exercise is to establish a rhythm, not to increase lung capacity.

Next, hold your breath to the mental count of two. Remember this should be done by means of the abdominal muscles, not by closing the throat.

Now, breathe out to the count of four. It may not be easy at first, but you are aiming to establish a situation where you are counting at a steady pace throughout the entire sequence.

Finally, hold your breath *out* for a count of two.

The sequence again in brief: *In* to the count of four; *hold* to the count of two; *out* to the count of four; *hold out* to the count of two. Repeat this sequence, increasing your practice time gradually each day, until it becomes fluid and trouble-free. Eventually, once begun, it will become quite automatic – your unconscious, given time to learn the sequence, will take it over and do the work for you.

During this exercise, you will find you take in more air than when breathing normally. This holds good even without straining, since most people tend to breathe in a very shallow manner. Increased oxygen in your lungs means an increase of oxygen in your blood. You have begun a minor biochemical reaction. The end result is improved relaxation.

The benefit does not end there. You are practising this

exercise in conjunction with conscious relaxation. Combine the two often enough and regularly enough and a curious psychological mechanism comes into play. It is a mechanism mentioned earlier in a different context – the mechanism of association.

Eventually (and Pavlov's basic research suggests fifty to seventy consecutive sessions should do the trick) your mind will firmly associate 2/4 breathing with relaxation. Once this happens, you have only to embark on the breathing sequence to produce relaxation via a conditioned reflex.

It is a particularly useful talent to develop, apart altogether from its occult benefits. When a crisis arises, you can fight panic with a breath, regain poise through a spontaneous 2/4 sequence. For the body and the mind are closely interlinked and when the first becomes relaxed, the second relaxes also.

Once you have achieved the art of relaxation, you have broken down the barrier between that vast sea of spiritual energy and yourself. Your next job is to provide the necessary channels for its flow.

Here we hit on a difficult concept. The channels are already there. They exist as inborn organs of the mind. But to bring them into conscious function requires time and effort. There is no real parallel on the physical plane. Your heart either beats or it doesn't. Your liver will work or it won't. And, Christian Barnard aside, there is very little you can do about this, indeed very little you need to do.

The nearest physical analogy I can think of is that of muscles. You were born with a full set, but they needed exercise to grow and still need it to function efficiently. The analogy is not perfect, but the psychic channels are at least a little like that.

If you are at all familiar with the Oriental systems, you may have come across the idea of chakras. If so, you will certainly have met the notion that Man is equipped with more than one body. This latter idea could become a complex study in itself. At the moment, however, it is fortunately possible to limit consideration to two bodies other than the physical. These are the etheric and the astral (or astro-mental).

Your etheric body is your invisible double. It interpenetrates

The Middle Pillar
Astro-Mental
Centres

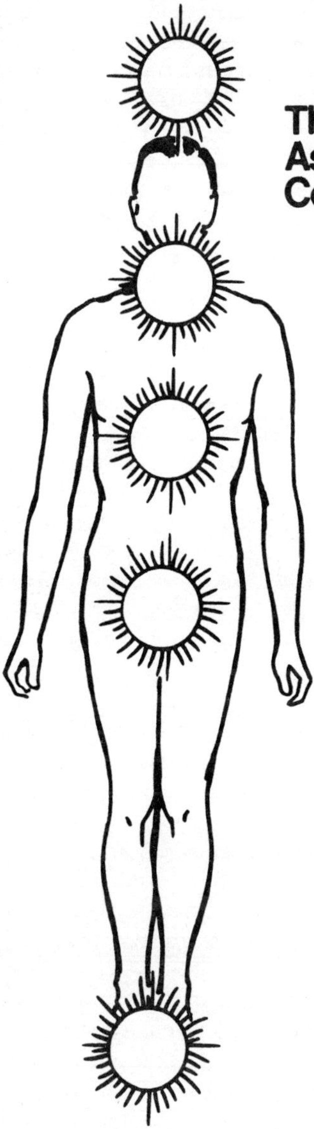

fig 1

your physical body and some schools of thought believe it is essentially a pattern of forces on which your physical body is built. It is closer to matter than to mind. That is to say it belongs to the material plane in the way that electricity and magnetism do. It seems to function as a link between your physical body and your mind.

Your astral body is a step beyond the etheric. And this step takes you into the realms of the psyche proper. The astral body is composed of mind-stuff; or, more accurately, imagination-stuff.

The chakras are 'nerve points' of the etheric body. They are closely linked on one hand to the spiritual channels of the higher bodies; and on the other to the glands and plexi of the physical.

Many of the Hatha Yoga exercises are designed to stimulate the chakras, thus producing beneficial effects on the physical body. The Western occultist will usually fight shy of this method. Without a guru on the spot to keep the chela out of trouble, it can be dangerous. So the Occidental magician turns his attention to the astral body. By working on it, he gets the same results eventually. The process is slower, but safer and there is plenty of time.

Please examine Fig. 1. It shows five important centres in the astral body. Each is linked with a chakra. Each is also linked with the Tree of Life as it is finally established in the aura of a Qabalist. Because of this, the centres are known collectively as The Middle Pillar. It is these Middle Pillar centres that you will have to bring from latent to actual functioning. This is how you can do so.

Assume your relaxation posture and go into the 2/4 breathing sequence. When this is going smoothly, visualize a sphere of brilliant white light hanging in space above the crown of your head. If you have ever watched the early morning sun breaking through mist or light cloud, you will have a perfect reference for the brilliant whiteness of the sphere.

As you visualize, vibrate the sounds *Eh-heh-yeh*.

Many of the grimoires make great play about *vibrating* the barbarous words of power. But few of them stop to give instructions on how the vibration is brought about. This has led to needless confusion, for the vibration of a sound is a simple knack gained with a little practice.

The best approach is to pitch your voice a shade lower than you would normally use and let the word originate at the back of the throat. Speak slowly and deliberately, experimenting until you can actually feel the vibration. This is neither difficult nor dramatic. All sound produces a vibration and it is only a question of intensifying it slightly.

The next part of the knack sounds a lot more difficult, but isn't. You must attempt to have the sound vibrate in a specific place, in this case at the centre of the imaginary sphere above your head. You will find you have only to keep your mind firmly on the sphere while repeating the name and the sounds will trigger there of their own accord.

This sparkling sphere of energy, experienced as imagination-stuff, established by an act of will, is your prime contact with the vast store of spiritual energy surrounding you. The sounds given, a phonetic of an ancient Hebrew name of God, also establish a link with the storehouse.

Nor is any of this mere dogma to be accepted as an act of faith. Once the sphere is established, you will feel the effects of the contact. Usually the sensation is a surge of energy and often a distinct tingling sensation is experienced. Like everything else, your contact is improved as it is more firmly established with practice.

Patience is a prerequisite of magical training, which tends to build at a stately pace. Take your time in establishing this sphere firmly. Keep up the exercise until you can visualize the energy source clearly. It will occur to you eventually that you are engaging in an exercise of auto-suggestion; and so you are. But it should become clear later that auto-suggestion is not the total answer. Results are too far-reaching.

When the first sphere is established to your satisfaction, move on to the next. Visualize a shaft of brilliant white light moving downwards from the sphere through the centre of your skull and blossoming into a second sphere of white light at your throat.

As this sphere is established, vibrate the sounds *Yeh-ho-vo-El-hoh-eem.*

With two spheres properly established, the shaft of light continues down to the solar plexus region and produces a third sphere. Here you should vibrate *Yeh-ho-vo-El-hoh-ah-vey-daas.*

Next you should extend the shaft to your genitals where a fourth sphere is established to the sounds *Shad-oy-El-chay.*

Finally comes the fifth sphere at your feet, built up by an act of imagination and reinforced by vibration of the sounds *Ah-do-noy-ha-Are-etz.*

Once you have achieved the full sequence, you will look, in your imagination, something like Fig. 1. The difference, if you have been visualizing properly, is that no illustration can convey the dynamic quality of those sparkling spheres.

Build the Middle Pillar in white light during the early stages of your training, which will take a period of weeks. When you have gained proficiency, build the spheres in colour. What colours you use depends on the books you've read, or rather, the books you've read and believed.

This is not so cynical as it sounds. Even the best sources vary. In *The Art of True Healing*, for instance, Israel Regardie, who is probably the greatest living authority on magic, ascribes the following colours to the spheres.

Crown – White
Throat – Lavender
Stomach – Red
Genitals – Blue
Feet – Russet

Those in the know are hard put to disagree with Regardie, whose prestige is enormous. At the same time, any magician past the apprentice stage tends to make a considered choice from the four colour scales of the Qabalah. Any conflict is more apparent than actual. A valve is not a transistor, but you can build a perfectly good radio set with either.

Since you are going to need the Qabalistic colour scales eventually, they are given in full as an appendix to this book. But in the interim, for the sake of simplicity and convenience, stay with the Regardie symbolism. Your metaphorical radio may be based on a cat's whisker, but what do you care so long as it picks up five-pound notes?

## CHAPTER FOUR

# THE £5-NOTE TRICK

Stand up and stretch your arms as far as they will go. Now congratulate yourself on having discovered the practical working limits of your aura.

In the stately days of Queen Victoria, men of science thought the aura was a myth. Today they generally accept there is indeed a weak electrical field surrounding the human body. But they have still a long way to go before agreement is reached with the occultists.

The magician, who enjoys structuring, divides this weak force-field into two – the inner and the outer auras. Together they envelop the body like an egg and most people find them quite impossible to detect. I can see the inner aura, but it isn't very interesting. It extends about an inch from the surface of the skin and looks for all the world like grey-blue cigarette smoke. It behaves like molten plastic. The only man I ever met who could see the outer aura turned out to be a liar. This is not to suggest that the outer aura does not exist. I have yet to meet anyone who has seen Poland, but Hitler's armies presumably invaded somewhere of that name in 1939.

Clairvoyants aver they can see colours in the outer aura. Some go so far as to say they can judge moods or diagnose ailments from these colours. If you have been doing the previous exercises with diligence, clairvoyant examination of your aura will reveal the Middle Pillar spheres strongly established.

At this stage, you are almost ready to try the five-pound note trick. All you lack is a little extra knowledge. Here again, it is knowledge of associations which have been accepted for so long that they have become synchronistic.

As I mentioned in the last chapter, you will eventually come to use the full system of the Qabalah. But here again, for speed and convenience, I propose to stick to Regardie's more simplified approach. In his suggested colour scheme for the Middle Pillar,

Regardie based his associations on the elements. For the actual magical working, he suggests seven astrological associations. You will find the full list in his excellent little book.* But the association necessary for money (and hence for five-pound notes) is the Sun.

Regardie gives a positive colour association of *orange* and a negative colour association of *yellow* or *gold*. The phonetic word of power is *Ye-ho-vo-El-hoh-ah-ve-da-as*. A negative association attracts something towards you. A positive association sends it out from you as a gift to someone else.

All of which brings you to the moment you've been waiting for – the full, detailed instructions for the five-pound note trick.

There are cosmic tides which make magic easier to work at certain times. Strictly speaking, you should learn and observe them. But since they would add a further complication to a complicated process, you can ignore them for your first experiment. You can let sheer effort take the place of skill.

Start on the first day of the month. Leave aside fifteen minutes to half an hour each morning and each evening. Determine not to miss a single day or night for the next four weeks – unless, that is, results come quicker than you thought.

Sit, or lie down, whichever you find most comfortable. Begin the 2/4 breathing sequence. If you have been practising as instructed, 2/4 breathing will trigger off the relaxation response. Should you notice any tension, get rid of it by the conscious relaxation process. A good clue to complete relaxation is that your body and limbs tend to feel heavy, so that any movement is a distinct effort.

Now activate the Middle Pillar centres by visualization and vibration of the words of power.

Having broken down the barriers by relaxation and set up the channels via Middle Pillar spheres, your next job is to circulate the power obtained throughout your aura.

There are a number of technical methods for doing this. One, which is both easy and effective, goes as follows. Throw your mind to the topmost sphere. On an outbreath, which, you recall,

* *The Art of True Healing*, published by Helios.

is being done to the count of four, visualize a sheet of light emanating from the sphere and travelling down the left side of your body. Try to feel the sensation as this light passes down the side of your head and on down your body, moving just beneath the skin and glowing through it. Imagine too that as the main sheet passes, it leaves a strong afterglow. The whole thing in some respects is like the sweep of the light arm on a radar screen.

As the light reaches your feet, it will, of course, become absorbed into the shining bottom sphere. In terms of your 2/4 breathing, the downward sweep took place to the count of four on an outbreath and the absorption into the lowest sphere lasts for a two count with the breath held outside the body.

On your next inbreath, again to the count of four, visualize the light travelling upwards, following a similar path along the right-hand side of your body until it reunites once more with the uppermost sphere for a count of two with breath retained.

Spelled out, the sequence seems complicated, but in practice it is easy enough and will soon become a fluid, semi-automatic movement of visualized light. Repeat the process until you can feel the effects of the flow (which probably will not be in less than half a dozen circuits).

Once this is achieved, set up a second circuit. This time the light should travel downwards over your face and the front of your body, returning upwards along your back. You will obviously have to visualize a broader beam, but otherwise the breathing sequence remains identical. Here again continue for at least half a dozen circuits.

Recapitulating briefly, you have at this stage broken down the barriers between yourself and the spiritual sea by relaxation. You have formed the channels for and transformers of power flow by activating the Middle Pillar. And you have circulated the power through your aura by rhythmical descent and ascent of light. You have, in short, charged your being with an unusual type of energy. It remains only to direct it.

Since your heart burns with desire for a five-pound note, it is necessary to attune yourself to a Sun (money) association. A Qabalist would use a single colour for both positive and negative operations, but since you are working, at least temporarily, on the simplified Regardie system, you will use the negative colour association. You will choose the negative since you wish the five-pound note to come to you, rather than go out to a friend.

Regardie's negative colours for the Sun are yellow or gold. You can strengthen the association in strictly common-sense terms, by working with the latter. Visualize the colour strongly. Feel it permeate your being until you reach the stage where, in your mind's eye, your entire aura glows with golden light. At this stage, only one more step is needed.

That final step is to visualize the arrival of the five-pound note. Picture the note clearly. Picture it in your possession. The exact circumstances of its arrival do not matter so long as you visualize with confidence, the sort of utter confidence you would experience if the money was actually in your pocket.

In theory it is perfectly possible to produce the required effect at a single attempt. In practice – and especially at first – it will be necessary to repeat the process. Regardie actually suggests repeating it twice a day, night and morning. Give yourself a month. If the trick has not worked by then, revise your technique.

After working with this method for a while, it becomes possible to simplify. An example will show you clearly what I mean.

Years ago, in some occultist publication, I read an article about the magical use of visualization. The author, whose name escapes me, suggested it was only necessary to visualize a situation clearly with intent and it came about. When he was late for an appointment, he had only to visualize a parking space at his destination and, lo!, one was always there awaiting him.

The theory seemed a bit far-fetched, but I tried it. Possibly his parking-space example swayed me. Parking at the time was not a major problem, but it was certainly a recurring irritation. I visualized furiously . . . and turned a minor irritation into a major problem. As sure as I visualized a space, I arrived to find no spaces open. When I forgot, I had at least an even money chance of getting parked.

At the time, I had no knowledge of synchronicity and only a

superficial knowledge of magic. Had it been otherwise, I might have spotted a clue – the recurrence of a negative effect.

As you perform the Middle Pillar exercises and their associated visualizations, you set up a synchronistic situation. The ritual has a meaning for you. And since there is confidence and belief behind it, whatever strange forces make synchronicity tick are directed in a positive manner.

But as I visualized for parking, I was setting up exactly the reverse situation. I did not believe it was going to work. The theory was ridiculous and the method lacked any element of drama. So synchronicity went into operation in the direction of my belief and made damn sure I could not park the car. The point is worth remembering: magic works in the direction of your belief, not necessarily in the direction of your intent.

After I learned to use the Middle Pillar, I tried the simpler parking trick again and found it worked. My inner attitude had been reversed.

## CHAPTER FIVE

# OCCULT ECCENTRICITIES

Returning from a stroll one summer afternoon, Mrs M walked through a copse and came upon a wood nymph.

Mrs M, widow of one of the best novelists Wales has managed to produce this century, was elderly, but there was nothing wrong with her eyesight. The entity, in the shape of a beautiful young girl with long brown legs and long blonde hair, dipped its toes in a pool beneath the trees.

I was very familiar with the spot. The pool was artificial, some centuries old, and disused. It was fed, via a sluice, from a little stream. The mechanism of the sluice was rusted and it is doubtful if it had been opened within living memory. Besides, an outlet in the bottom of the pool remained free: rainwater failed to collect, even in the sharpest downpour.

Mrs M knew all this as well as I did. Yet the pool, she said, was brim-full of crystal water when she saw it.

Did she, I asked, say anything to the creature?

Mrs M looked shocked. 'Good heavens no! It certainly wasn't my place to speak to such an etherial being.' She paused, then added, 'She had such a lovely aura.'

I had never seen a wood nymph and the thought of talking to someone who had met one such a short time before excited me enormously. I tried to guess what my own reactions would have been in the circumstances. 'If you didn't speak to her, what *did* you do?'

Mrs M's calm eyes focused on my own and a faint expression of surprise crossed her features. 'I was rather late for tea,' she said, 'so I walked on down to the house . . .'

In fiction, people faced suddenly by the occult behave in all sorts of dramatic ways. In life – at least so far as my experience goes – their behaviour is simply eccentric. Who, faced with a wood nymph, would worry about being late for tea? Only, one might imagine, such a civilized and genteel lady as Mrs M. But one would be wrong. Swept up in the experience of the praeternatural, the varieties of human reaction seem endless.

On Easter Sunday, a friend arrived to say he had seen a leprechaun in the late afternoon or early evening of Good Friday. Curiously enough, the apparition had appeared quite close to the spot where Mrs M came across her wood nymph.

For some reason, wood nymphs are a trifle more believable than leprechauns and I was immediately convinced my friend was joking. But it soon became obvious that he was not.

He was planting trees in the little wood when a sound caused him to look up. Sitting on a stump, watching him with interest, was a leprechaun – or, at least, something very strange.

It may be as well to explain at this stage that the wood in question is on private property in Ireland, considerably distant from the road. It is not a spot where one might expect to find casual callers.

The creature on the stump was small, masculine and old. In telling me about it, my friend mentioned that at first glance, he assumed it was a child (a four- or five-year-old). But it was quite close and the features were those of a little old man. The clothing was all wrong too. Modern children tend to wear light colours. This soul had clothed himself in dark, rough homespun.

To those who have never seen one, leprechauns are fiction, foolishness or lunacy. But such convictions are difficult to maintain when faced by a creature who looks like a leprechaun in an Irish wood. All the ancient folklore about the Little People comes flooding back. A suspicion creeps in: could so many generations of the Irish have believed in leprechauns if there wasn't *something* behind it? Perhaps some subtle vibrations in the air of Ireland open the eyes to an Otherworld where fantasies become reality?

My friend is no fool. (He holds an M.A. from Oxford.) Although neither a psychic nor a mystic, he had enough self-confidence to believe the evidence of his own eyes. He concluded that, unlikely though the situation might be, he was looking at a leprechaun. He also concluded that any searching analysis of the experience would have to wait. Just then the important thing was to establish contact.

With some vague notion that the Little People must speak Gaelic, he searched his limited vocabulary of that language and came up with the only phrase he knew that seemed even vaguely appropriate.

My friend greeted the leprechaun with the words, *'Erin go bra!'*

At this point, the account becomes less than clear. It may be that the leprechaun replied – for it made some sound – but the words were indistinct or the language strange. In any case, my friend was unable to communicate. He became excited, so that, later, he was unable to recall exactly what he said. But he said something, and waved his arms.

There were two frisky terriers in the vicinity. They belonged to my friend and, bored by his tree-planting activities, had wandered off in search of rats or rabbits. Now, however, they began to race back, barking, attracted by the noise.

My friend heard them and turned to shout, 'Keep back! Keep back!' He wanted no dogs worrying his leprechaun. The dogs stopped obediently, but when my friend turned again, the leprechaun had vanished. Had he studied folklore, he might have remembered the tradition that, to catch a leprechaun, you must never, never take your eyes off him . . .

How much credibility can we place on such stories? I knew Mrs M only a short time, but she struck me as a scrupulously honest woman. She was serious-minded and perceptive, interested in the occult, but hardly credulous. None of these qualities guarantees immunity from hallucination, but the essence of hallucination for the insane is its fascination. You do not simply leave your hallucination behind because you are a little late for tea.

My friend is a slightly different case, for he was not above playing an occasional practical joke. Was he joking in this case? I doubt it. The trouble with reporting you have seen a leprechaun or wood nymph is that the joke's on you. People assume, almost as a matter of course, that you are being silly, or perhaps mad.

Since these very curious manifestations took place, I have discovered that at least two pieces of alleged *physical* evidence of leprechauns exist in Ireland. One is a tiny shoe, hand-stitched and beautifully made to fit a mature (but tiny) foot. The other is a pair of gloves, discovered packed into a walnut shell and walled into the mortar of an old house.

Examination of these artifacts soon shows they were not designed for children: the proportions are all wrong. If we leave the Little People out of our considerations for a moment, we fall back on two possibilities – they were made for midgets or as curios. Midgets are rare, curios less so. People do still engrave the Lord's Prayer on the head of a pin.

But what makes these little curios so very unlikely is the material of which they are made. The shoe has some of the properties of leather, but is not leather. The gloves are stranger still, having the feel of silk and the strength of nylon, but being, in fact, neither. If we were talking of the modern age, we might speculate that the material was a synthetic. The shoe was, however, discovered prior to the development of modern synthetics. The gloves, while a much more recent discovery, were walled up for more than half a century.

Fascinating though such evidence may be, I tend to believe Mrs M and my friend for less tangible reasons. They behaved in an eccentric manner. One went home for tea, the other waved his arms and shouted, *'Erin go bra!'* Such odd reactions in the face of the unknown have, to me, an absolutely genuine ring about them. They are not exactly what I would do in similar circumstances, but they are the *type of thing* that I would do.

I am very much aware how easily eccentricity manifests in circumstances like these, for once I found myself trying to defeat a lie-detector with a nursery rhyme. And there is nothing more eccentric than that!

Yoga, to the West, means Hatha Yoga. But there are other branches of this great Oriental system. One of them is Mantra Yoga and it is probably the least understood Way of Union with the One.

A mantra is a sound, or series of sounds, used as an aid to meditation. It is often thought of as the Oriental counterpart of the Western words of power, but this is not altogether true. The immediate mechanics of the two are different. As explained earlier, words of power are vibrated in the West to open psychic channels. They can also be used to bring semi-autonomous complexes (the new name for spirits) to the surface of consciousness. At their most spectacular level, they can evoke the archetypes (gods) themselves. A mantra does something very different. Properly used, it sets up a closed circuit in the mind, forcing the attention in a specific direction, opening the way to ecstatic experience..

There are many examples of a mantra. The simplest and most widely known is *Om*. 'Om' is a written symbol of the basic background vibration of the universe. This is a lot less esoteric than it may appear. If you find a quiet spot, still your mind and listen, you can hear the vibration for yourself. Although perhaps 'hear' is the wrong word. You will experience the vibration largely as sound, but part of it will be felt rather than heard; and a further part will be largely psychic in origin.

The vibration is worth listening for. It gives the key to the mystery of pronouncing Om. You will find the mantra is hummed rather than spoken. The best approach is to break the word into three syllables: *Aw-uh-mmmm*.

Om is frequently expanded into a sonorous phrase which is also widely used as a mantra – *Om mani padme hum*. If you take the subjective viewpoint, the words are translated 'Hail to the jewel in the lotus'. As such they salute the essence of the uppermost sphere in our diagram of the psychic channels. In the West, this sphere is referred to Kether on the Tree of Life. In the East, it is associated with the chakra named The Thousand-Petalled Lotus. Should you prefer an objective (i.e. cosmic) viewpoint, a better translation of the manta might be 'Hail to Thee the Ever-Becoming One'.

On its own, Om is repeated with a rise-and-fall rhythm, like a sine graph. The full phrase, however, will give you a better example of the essentially circular nature of a mantra. In visual terms, a mantra is a ring of elephants or a snake swallowing its own tail.

Try repeating *Om mani padme hum* a few times. Pace the words evenly, half humming the natural rhythm of the phrase.

You will soon find that the final *hummmm* blends into the initial *aummmmm* to form an integrated circular sequence.

This is a natural sequence in a mantra and the key to its effect. If you have ever been plagued by a tune that you can't get out of your head, you will know what the effect is like. With a mantra, however, you remain in control of the situation.

To establish the closed circuit, repeat the mantra aloud, slowly and evenly. Make sure there is a distinct pause between each repetition. Now speed up. Close the pause down gradually until you are repeating a single circular phrase. The next step is to let your voice die away, taking up the mantra mentally. Do this smoothly, so that it seems the mantra, which began as a spoken phrase, is gradually absorbed into the mind. Continue to speed up until you have reached the stage where the mantra is spinning mentally. At this stage, you will find it continues, as it were, of its own accord. In fact the spin has been taken up by your unconscious mind.

As is the case with most magical techniques, it is inadvisable to overdo the practice in the early stages. Build up your efficiency at a slow and steady rate, gradually increasing the length of time you keep the mantra spinning.

The Yoga adept trains his concentration to a point where he can fix attention on a single thing for incredibly long periods of time. He forces all other considerations, all other thoughts, from his mind. He holds to one thing and waits.

What he waits for is absorption. As he forced out all distractions, he moved towards a simple, basic duality – the observer and the observed. But when he reaches the duality and holds it, a strange thing happens: the observer ceases to differentiate between itself and the observed. The Yogi becomes his thought and since his thought is single,. the Yogi becomes single too. He has merged with the focus of attention. He has become One.

The experience is not easy to achieve, but the mantra is a powerful technique for forcing the mind in the required direction. Its spin throws off intruding thoughts until the man becomes the mantra.

It is seldom wise to start something you can't stop. Stopping a spinning mantra requires a reversal of the process which began it in the first place. Slow the spin gradually, then externalize the mantra by speaking it aloud. Slow further until the circle is broken by ever-lengthening pauses, then stop.

*Om mani padme hum* is Indian in origin, forming part of Buddhist practice. So many excellent mantras have come out of India that Westerners tend to conclude that great continent has a monopoly on the product. But this is not so. Many cults in many countries have coined phrases which act as mantras. A useful example from the Middle East is *Hua allahu alazi lailaha illa Hua* (He is the One God and there is no other God but He).

A lie-detector is a machine designed to measure certain subtle changes in the human body. It works because mind and body are very closely interlinked. We can maintain a poker face while we tell a brazen lie, but we cannot control a host of tiny physical symptoms of our untruth. We cannot, for instance, halt the slight rise in blood pressure, the minute tension of the muscles, the faint stimulation of the sweat glands.

These changes pass unnoticed in the average man unless quite delicate measuring machinery is used. One of the simplest forms of such measuring machinery is a device which meters the rate at which the skin conducts electricity. This rate, oddly enough, varies with our emotional state. A machine measuring the variations is an efficient enough lie-detector, although perhaps 'emotion detector' would be a better term.

In a room used for the meetings of an esoteric organisation which interested me, I sat having my emotions measured. After a while, the success of the machine began to annoy me. Finally it became a challenge. I decided to apply the mantra principle in the hope of deadening my reactions. I succeeded totally.

The 'mantra' used was more familiar than those quoted from India and the Middle East. It ran,

> Twinkle, twinkle, little star,
> How I wonder what you are,
> Up above the world so high,
> Like a diamond in the sky.

Eccentric reactions . . . eccentric techniques. My funny little mantra is not the only odd thing to produce results. There is, for instance, a very unlikely technique designed to raise spirits which I have yet to see fail. By raising spirits, I mean, of course, the alleviation of depression.

Seat your (depressed) patient in a chair facing you and tell him to follow instructions. If you can persuade him to relax a little, it helps the thing along, but for once relaxation is not vital.

Point to the wall on your right and tell him to look at it, then look back at you. When he does, say, 'Thank you.'

In turn, point to each of the other walls in the room, the floor and the ceiling. 'Now look at that wall . . . thank you.'

Have him look at each wall twice, then shift into second gear. This time ask that he not only looks at the wall, but imagines it saying hello to him. 'Have this wall say "Hello, John".' When he does so, thank him and continue the sequence through with walls, floor and ceiling.

Next time round is almost a repeat, except that now the emphasis is on the imaginary 'Hello'. Show him what you mean by your inflection. Instead of the straightforward 'Hello, John', he should imagine the Big Hello, the public relations man's emphatic intonation of delight: '*Hell*-o, John.'

When he has finished the sequence, have him imagine all the walls, the floor and ceiling greeting him simultaneously in warmest tones. He'll find at this stage the depression has evaporated.

## CHAPTER SIX

# GOLD AND GHOSTS

Virtually anything can be put to a magical use. I learned this lesson not from a magician, but from a BBC newsreader. Aware of my interest in oddities, he drew me away from the main body of a spirited party and whispered, 'I can tell you what to do with your coathangers . . .'

It is not, unfortunately, a case of any old coathanger. What you need are the wire ones laundries use to send back your dry-cleaning. If you have a look in the wardrobe now, chances are you'll find half a dozen you've saved up for emergencies. Take two and accept the fact that you are about to ruin them as far as hanging clothes is concerned. As against that, you are about to build a very versatile magical weapon.

First, untwist the coathanger. You will find it is comprised of a single piece of wire twisted together at the hook. Straighten the whole thing out as best you can.

You will find it straightens reasonably well, except for the hook part which you can safely ignore. Trim the difficult ends off with wire-cutters and bend the remainder into an L shape. The shorter leg of the L should be quite short, somewhere around the 6 inches to 8 inches mark. Exact size is not critical, but since you will be using this end as a hand grip, make sure it will be comfortable.

When you have completed the L, untwist the second coathanger and manufacture a duplicate of the first. Together they form an instrument that will detect water, gold or ghosts.

Don, my friend from the BBC, discovered the magical use of coathangers from an unlikely source. A Major in the Royal Engineers had developed them as an implement for water divining. Unlike the common hazel twig, he claimed the coathangers could detect metals and ceramics as well as water.

At the time, Don was something of a sceptic. But he followed the Major's instructions and found, to his surprise, he had charted the location of an Army underground water tank.

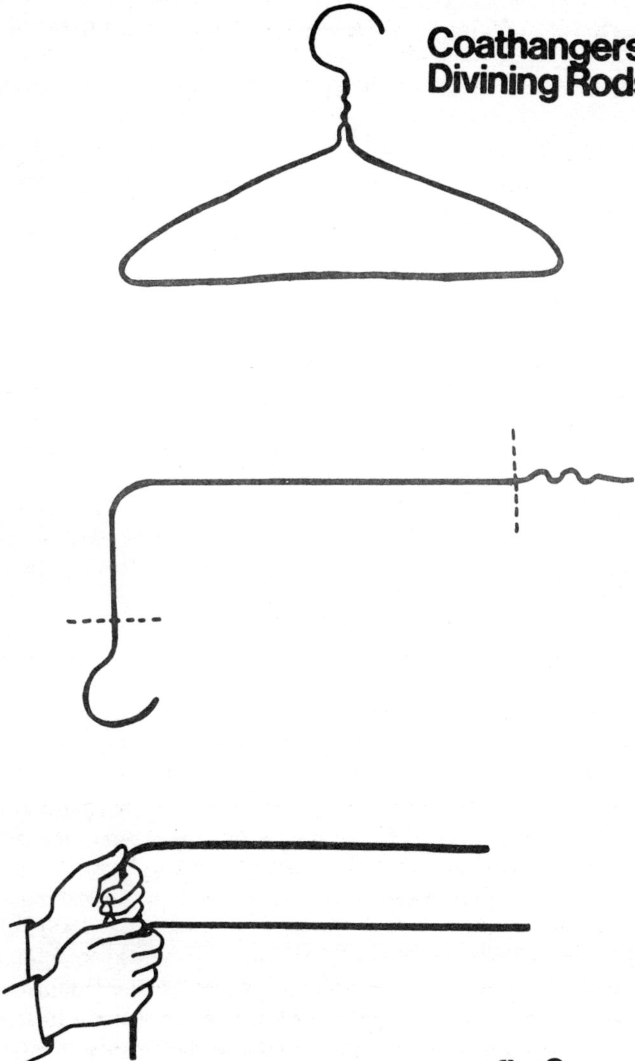

**Coathangers as Divining Rods**

fig 2

Subsequent experiments convinced him his talent with the coathangers was not unique. Most people could work them once they knew how.

The *modus operandi* is simplicity itself. Hold the coathangers by the short leg of the L. Arrange the longer arms so that they are pointing away from you and parallel to one another like railway tracks. Hold the hangers gently, so that the longer arms have free play. Then walk. As you pass over water, the long arms of the coathangers will swing together and cross.

Like so much magical activity, there is an enormous amount of suggestion involved in operating the coathangers. Few people want to dig wells, so your first experiments will probably be the 'detection' of a bowl of water on the kitchen floor. As you pass over the bowl, the wires will cross simply because you have suggested to your unconscious that they should.

The next most common form of experiment, detecting underground drains or wastepipes, is only a little more sophisticated. Here again, the wires will cross easily enough. But here again, most people are perfectly well aware of where the drains are located. Even if you have never thought of it consciously, logic could still provide you with the most likely path of an outlet and the unconscious mind is far from stupid.

When I became reasonably proficient with the method, I taught the system to three unquestioning novices. To determine how far suggestion went, I gave them a list of purely arbitrary rules. I told them initially that if a penny was held in the hand, the wires would cross when held above a penny on the floor. And so they did. I then suggested that if the penny in the hand was changed for a sixpence, the wires would cross over another sixpence, but swing outwards if held above a penny since copper and silver were 'antagonistic' metals. Again the coathangers behaved as predicted.

Finally, I stretched credibility to the limit. I would *imagine* a bowl of water on a certain (well-defined) spot on the floor. The wires would cross as they picked up this 'thought-form'. In two cases they did. In the third, nothing happened. The girl holding the wires told me she thought the whole business of 'thought-forms' was nonsense.

In face of this, there would seem to be little doubt that the unconscious mind operates the wires. This is to say, you have not constructed a machine which picks up subtle emanations from water, silver, copper or dubious thought-forms. But despite the element of suggestion, the coathangers cannot be dismissed as an example of a psychological novelty. Nor can the pendulum, which is a slightly more complicated way of achieving the same results.

You can make a pendulum quite easily. Simply tie a weight on to a piece of thread. But before embarking on experiments, it is necessary to determine for yourself the 'wavelength' of various items. A divining pendulum will make one of two movements – backwards and forwards, or in a circle. Traditionally, a pendulum of the correct length will swing backwards and forwards if held over the hand of a man; and describe a circular movement if held over the hand of a woman. This association is so strongly established that you will often find the pendulum used to determine the sex of an unborn child. How successful the method is in practice I have no idea. But I know it works for other things.

Before you can start using the pendulum, you need to decide what you want to use it for. Let us suppose like the Faustian adepts you wish to find gold. Take the handiest piece – a wedding ring or similar piece of jewellery – and hold the pendulum over it. The chances are that absolutely nothing will happen. Now slowly adjust the length of the thread, pausing frequently. Sooner or later you will find a length at which the pendulum describes a circle over the gold. Mark this length on the thread.

If you can resist the urge to go prospecting right away, you can make a multi-purpose pendulum. Simply repeat the process with, say, tin, copper and silver, marking the length each time.

The one danger in the process is self-deception. Make no attempt to move the pendulum yourself: just let things happen. Like the coathangers, the pendulum is a tap to your unconscious mind. Prepare it properly. The results are well worth the effort.

Where the pendulum scores in practice is that it does not need to be held over an object to determine its presence. Try this trick and, as the ads say in America, astound your friends.

Have someone hide a gold object somewhere in a room. You are not engaged in conjuring, so don't try to listen or work out where the item might be. Once it is safely stowed away, come in with your pendulum. (It goes without saying that the pendulum should be adjusted to the gold 'wavelength'.)

Take up a position near the door. Hold the pendulum in your left hand and set it swinging to and fro. Now hold out your right hand and sight along it as if you were pointing. Move your right hand slowly and systematically so that eventually it will have pointed to all parts of the room. At some stage in this manoeuvre, you will find the pendulum changes its swing into a circle. When this happens, you are pointing at the object.

I had better come right out and admit that while almost everyone can work the coathangers, the trick with the pendulum seems to call for a special talent. But even here the talent is far from rare. From my own experiments, I would conclude that the number of people able to find hidden objects in this way is well over fifty per cent.

Once you have had a few practice runs, a variety of uses for both wires and pendulum will suggest themselves. One that may not occur to you is ghost hunting.

We had finished dinner in one of Ireland's most delightful stately homes. It was snowing heavily outside, but a huge log fire in the library kept the chill at bay. Our hostess, who was interested in such things, had just told us that the house was haunted.

The information could not have fallen on more delighted ears. My companions included my dear friend Desmond, a Theosophist and authority on flying saucers, and Kevin, whose past experiences had included involuntary etheric projection.

The ghost was a Grey Lady, an unhappy shade who flitted through the corridors without, apparently, doing a great deal of harm to anyone. According to Sybil Leeke, who once investigated the phenomenon, she was strongly associated with a particular room.

Had our hostess actually seen the ghost herself? She stared into the fire and nodded. The Grey Lady might be a ghost, but she was certainly not a myth.

We retired from the library to pace the carpeted corridors. None of us were particularly sensitive that night, for no ghost appeared. We asked out hostess if we could see the haunted room. At that stage she suggested an experiment. None of us had been to the house before. None of us knew which of the many rooms was associated with the ghost. Why not test our sensitivity to atmosphere and find it for ourselves?

We tried, but we did not succeed. When inspiration had almost run its course, Desmond suggested using a pendulum. The butler appeared bearing thread and a weight on a silver tray. We constructed our pendulum. No one knew if ghosts had a specific wavelength, but we set it to react when brought close to a woman and hoped the Grey Lady had not lost her femininity along with her life.

It took twenty minutes before Helen found a room in which the pendulum reacted madly.

'Is this it?' she asked.

Our hostess nodded.

The coathangers too will pick up ghosts, at least those ghosts which stand still long enough to be picked up. Our own home developed a cold spot which a clairvoyant diagnosed as 'an elemental trapped in a cone of force'. We accepted the diagnosis and learned to live with the elemental.

One evening when some friends were amusing themselves with the coathangers, we suggested trying them out in the corner where out house elemental lived. They did so and an odd thing happened. Instead of crossing, the wires went into reverse, swinging outwards. It seemed our elemental equated with some form of negative energy.

With pendulum and coathangers, we have come full circle to the moving glass. A discussion of theory is the next step and then, hopefully, on to more important things.

But before we leave Low Magic, it is interesting to take notice of a device which, although bordering on High Magic because of its use, is nonetheless in the same category as the instruments described in this chapter. I discovered the device when introduced to Mr O, a Dublin homoeopathist. He used, he said, a black box to diagnose illness in his patients. The 'black box', as it happened, turned out not to be a box at all, although it was certainly black. It was, in fact, a solid block of wood with a rubber membrane stretched on top. The whole thing was small enough to slip comfortably into the pocket, not very much larger than a packet of cigarettes.

When diagnosing, Mr O had the patient stand in front of him. He would then hold the block aimed, so to speak, at the patient's head and begin to stroke the membrane lightly. As he did so, he would lower the device slowly, covering the whole of the body. As soon as he had reached the seat of the illness, he found that he could no longer stroke the membrane smoothly. It crinkled beneath his fingers.

This is a very specialist use for a tap to the unconscious. Although Mr O could see no reason why anyone should fail to be able to use his black box, the fact remained that very few could do so.

Whether your unconscious has a gift for diagnosis is something you can only discover by experiment. A 'black box' is easy enough to make. But be extra careful not to take your experiments too far. A lot of patients have died from an acute attack of self-appointed healers.

## CHAPTER SEVEN

# MAGIC AND MIND

You've learned a lot about Low Magic. Now the time has come to evaluate. For Low Magic, despite the light-hearted tone of earlier chapters, is important. Some of its basic principles can lead you to High Magic, and High Magic can lead you to levels the man in the street will not dream of.

The one common denominator in every example of magic so far mentioned is mind. Even if you care to broaden the scope of your survey, you will find this holds good. A love potion may be chemical (or, more usually, bio-chemical) in composition, but it is designed to change the mind of the person who imbibes it. A talisman must first be charged. And this is done, one way or another, by a mental operation. (The simplest method I know is to activate the Middle Pillar, circulate the force, then, by an act of visualization, pour it into the chosen object. The operation requires fairly intense concentration, but provided you avoid synthetics, the object will hold the charge for quite a time.) Elemental servants, which arise from an operation not only low but grey, are conjured not from space, but from the psyche.

As I said in the early stages, all magic works from the inside out. There is another, more familiar, system which works the same way. That system is psychology. Once you begin to study psychology and magic side by side, some far-reaching parallels emerge.

Psychology postulates dimensions of reality other than the physical. Collectively these dimensions are known as the psyche. The conscious mind forms only a part of the psyche, and a small part at that, but it can make contact with, and is influenced by, other parts. Magic also postulates dimensions of reality other than the physical. Collectively they are known as the Inner Planes. Again the conscious mind may contact them and be influenced by them.

In psychology we learn of certain extra-physical energies.

Libido is an example from the Freudian school. The psychiatrist, whose interest lies in healing, stresses the importance of clearing the channels for these energies if the patient is to lead a full and happy life. The magician concurs, with only a slight difference in terminology. He thinks of the energies as spiritual or psychic in the non-psychological sense of the word. For centuries the magician has observed possession, the taking over of a human personality by some non-physical entity. In the unhappiest cases, the entity showed evil characteristics and was consequently considered Satanic or demonic. Unless stopped by exorcism, possession of this type frequently led to the death of the human host. A few years ago, I sat in a courtroom listening to a psychiatrist giving evidence about a patient who was schizophrenic. The patient had felt himself controlled by demons. Eventually his own personality disintegrated altogether and he committed suicide.

The magician speaks of spirits. The psychologist formulates theories about 'semi-autonomous complexes', constellations of psychic energy which behave as personalities in their own right and exhibit disquieting traits of independence.

The magician deals with gods, superhuman entities whose very presence fills him with awe. The psychologist talks of archetypes, dominants of the collective unconscious which exhibit a numenous, awe-inspiring quality.

Jung once perceptively remarked that it was a fruitless business denying the reality of the gods when you could better spend your time studying certain forces which behave exactly as the gods were reputed to behave.

A cardinal rule of magic is 'Know thyself'. A (Freudian) psychiatrist undergoes analysis as part of his training.

The magician, particularly the Qabalist, will undertake astral journeys in order to achieve sufficient balance to allow spiritual forces to flow through him. Jungians use the virtually identical technique of creative imagination in an attempt to integrate the psyche.

Freud's initial experiments involved hypnosis, a very ancient occult technique sometimes known as 'Fascination' and sometimes as the 'Evil Eye'.

The magician forms a very curious, almost telepathic relationship with his apprentice. The psychiatrist seeks rapport with his patients, and is often bemused by apparent instances of telepathy.

This is not designed to be an exhaustive list of parallels, but I think by now I have given enough to support my viewpoint that *magic is an archaic system of psychology.*

You are now equipped with a definition of magic. But like so many definitions of magic, this one has its drawbacks.

Psychology means simply the study of the mind. Unfortunately most of us tend to think of it as the *current* study of the mind, with the unconscious corollary that modern psychology must be correct in its conclusions. This is not so. Modern psychology is neither an exact science nor a complete one. And its only really widespread applications are in the fields of healing (psychiatry) and manipulation (advertising and propaganda).

The fact that there are only two practical applications at the moment does not mean there can be no more. Jung's theory of synchronicity points to a third. So will the current parapsychological experiments whenever it is realized that parapsychology is a false subdivision and this fascinating field should really form part and parcel of an overall psychology.

The second major drawback is the use of the word 'archaic'. Although conveying the ancient lineage of magic to perfection, it carries emotional overtones of uselessness. And the danger also arises of thinking of magic as primitive. Nothing could be further from the facts. To underline this, I will now make an interim amendment to my definition: *Magic is an archaic system of psychology – and a damn good one!*

In building a case for my original definition, it was necessary to stress the parallels between magic and modern psychology. To build a case for the amendment, I have to stress the differences. The heart of these differences lies in how you answer the age-old riddle of the chicken and the egg. In this instance, the chicken is the psyche and the egg the brain.

Modern psychology pays lip service to the idea that the psyche is real, but makes the tacit assumption that it is somehow less real than the brain. The Behaviourist School, now gaining in ascendancy, is one of the worst offenders. Every psychic experience can be (at least potentially) explained in terms of brain function. Damage the brain and you damage the mind. Stimulate the brain – through drugs or electrodes – and you stimulate the mind.

Victorian speculation on the subject has left a hangover. There is at the back of most psychological theory the woolly notion that the brain gives off mind as a kettle gives off steam, or radium gives off radioactivity. At best, the psychologist admits mind and brain are coexistent and interacting. The idea of a pre-existent mind usually produces a feeling of revulsion.

This viewpoint grossly limits psychological speculation. Semi-autonomous complexes exhibit personality characteristics. Sometimes one can take over completely from the normal personality. But where does the normal personality go when this happens? To a psychologist, this question is ludicrous. It remains ludicrous even when twin personalities alternate.

The notion that mind is totally dependent on the brain also rules out psychological speculation on the possibility and nature of life after death. Such speculation is left to theologians, who usually make a consistent mess of it. Even Jung, in his commentary on the *Tibetan Book of the Dead*, was careful not to go too far. You can read it from beginning to end without discovering whether he actually believed in life after death.

But to the magician, the chicken comes before the egg. The brain is an excellent computer in a fully-automated factory. It was built and is operated by the man in charge.

If you hold to this analogy, you will see that it explains observable facts just as well as the psychologists' conclusions. Remember that the person operating the factory is hidden from you. You can see only the factory and the actions of its machinery.

Damage the computer and the machinery breaks down. You have not, of course, damaged the man who owns it, but you might be tempted to draw that conclusion. If you interfere with the computer's delicate wiring, the production process goes haywire. But this does not mean that the operator has gone insane. Scramble the intercom and the man in charge appears to talk nonsense. But this is the fault of the intercom, not the man.

Regrettably, we can see only the body, never the mind that controls it. We can communicate only through verbal symbols, never directly. We meet lunatics and corpses and make certain assumptions about the mind, or lack of mind, behind them. There is at least a fifty per cent chance that these assumptions are wrong.

While the magician has laid his money squarely on the chicken, the matter does not end there. The magical theory of mind is complex and just as difficult to explain as the psychological.

First, the magician sees a continuity between the psyche and the physical world. One shades into the other with no really clear dividing line. He will go so far as to say that mind and matter are essentially the same thing,' or at least different manifestations of the same thing.

When someone told Chesterton coal and diamonds were the same, he is reputed to have replied, 'Any fool can see they aren't!' Yet the magician's notions are not quite so daft as they seem.

We are accustomed to physicists claiming that the chair we sit on is not solid. Equally, we are accustomed to behaving as if it was. If physics teaches anything at all, it is the certain fact that common sense is worthless for the task of getting to grips with reality.

Common sense tells us that no object can be in two places at once. Physics tells us an electron can. Physics also tells us that mesons *can* live only for a millionth of a second . . . and yet *do* exist for minutes, sometimes hours. Their energy content seems to distort time.

Since Einstein, physics has begun to form a picture of the universe in terms of energy or energies. With each fresh discovery, this picture grows uncomfortably close to that of the magician.

If you draw a spectrum, shading gradually from white to black, label one end 'Mind', the other 'Matter' and entitle the whole thing 'Energy', you have the magical picture. I fancy that

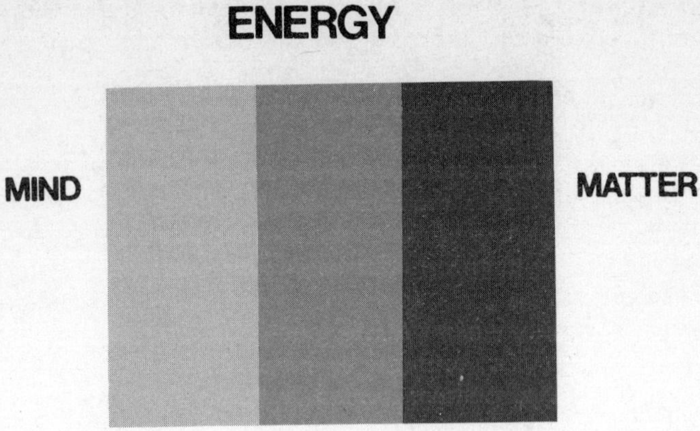


fig 3

if psychology ever gets together with physics, the scientists will draw a similar diagram.

Once you accept the magical viewpoint of psychology, a lot of old ideas take on a new lease of life. It is no longer superstition (or science-fiction) to consider the possibility of alien dimensions. Nor should you assume these dimensions cannot affect our own.

Magicians have through the ages claimed contact with other, non-physical worlds, have claimed such worlds are fountainheads of knowledge, power and wisdom. Put baldly, it seems fiction. But it is only a very short step beyond the present boundaries of orthodox depth psychology.

Alien contacts . . . alien wisdom. It begins to look as if we are embarking on a very romantic adventure, you and I. And so we are.

It may also look a little frightening. And so it can be. Before venturing into the realms of High Magic, which is largely concerned with establishing lines of communication with these other worlds and their inhabitants, it might be as well to examine the broad sweep of occult cosmology. It could be a comfort to you should things get tough.

CHAPTER EIGHT

# GROUND-PLAN OF THE UNIVERSE

> In the beginning God created the heaven and the earth.
> And the earth was without form and void: and darkness was upon the face of the deep.
> And the Spirit of God moved upon the face of the waters.
> And God said, Let there be light: and there was light.
> And God saw the light, that it was good: and God divided the light from the darkness.

That's how it all started, according to *Genesis*. At one time you might have taken the words as literal truth. Perhaps you still do, although it has become fashionable these days to dismiss the whole creation story as pure fiction. The magician, an unfashionable figure, does not dismiss *Genesis* as fiction. But he does not accept it literally either. Instead, he asks questions. One of the big ones is, What do you mean by God?

For an answer, he turns not to the Old Testament, but to an equally interesting Hebrew work, the Holy Qabalah. Unlike Genesis, the Qabalah does not define a starting point. In the beginning, before the beginning and after the beginning, there is, was and always will be existence. But there need not necessarily be manifest existence. Immediately we are in deep waters. The Qabalah is not easy to understand.

As an arbitrary starting point, you might like to consider the idea of negative existence – or, as the Qabalists refer to it, the Great Unmanifest.

There is very little you can say about the Great Unmanifest. Your existence is positive in nature: and so is everything you know. Words like 'negative existence' have no real meaning, because they refer to something beyond your experience. And something which, by its very nature, must remain beyond your experience. The very best you can do is follow the example of the Hindu who describes the Supreme Deity as 'Not This – Not That'.

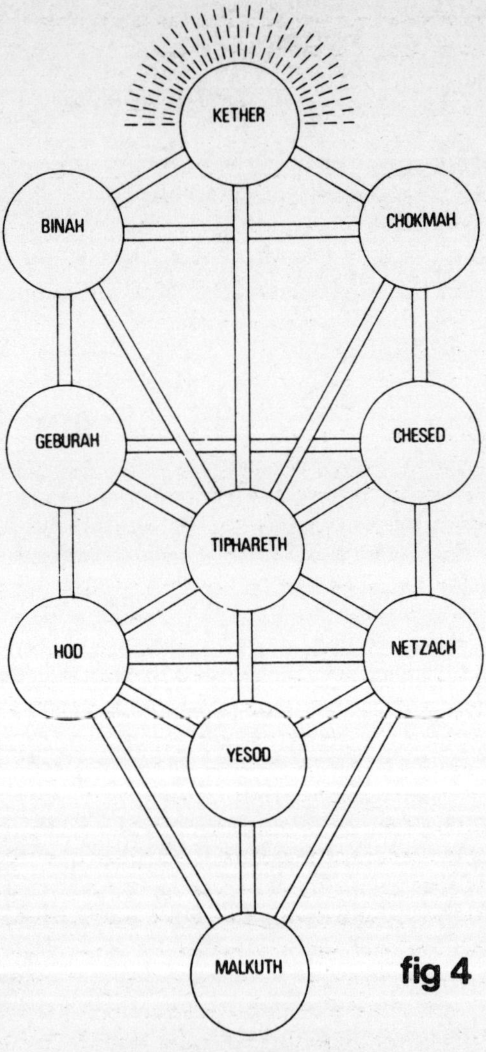


fig 4

**The Tree of Life**

However little we can say about the Great Unmanifest, we can at least know one thing: somewhere along the line there was a change. Positive existence came into being.

To the Qabalist, positive existence came into being with Kether. The essential fact of Kether is raw existence. The essence of the sphere is unity. While we could make no speculation about the Great Unmanifest, we can make every speculation about Kether. But each speculation will be equally true and false, because as unity, Kether is beyond all contradiction. Any terms applied to Kether are symbolic. Perhaps the best symbol is the number one.

As one, coupled with zero (the Great Unmanifest) forms the potential of every number, so Kether, contrasted against the backdrop of negative existence, forms the potential of duality. The Qabalist thinks of the situation in terms of pressure. The primordial unity of Kether develops self-awareness . . . and consequently becomes two. The Chokmah state is born.

Chokmah is the great positive masculine force of the universe. And since we are now firmly in the realms of duality, its very existence postulates its complementary. Thus Chokmah begets Binah.

It would be a mistake to assume that Kether, Chokmah and Binah are God, or gods, or even the Trinity. Equally it would be a mistake to assume they are not. Everything depends on your viewpoint. At one level of development, a fact may be experienced as a force. At another level as a god. The fact does not change, only the viewpoint.

From Binah, the Supernal Mother, springs a semblance of stability. The three primordial spheres are balanced . . . for a time. But manifestation is far from complete. The pressure is still there. The spheres reflect themselves on another level. Chesed, Geburah and Tiphareth are born.

Chesed is, among other things, the force of growth. Geburah is the force, or rather principle, of destruction. Together they represent progress, the building up and the breaking down, eternally co-existent principles. Tiphareth is the state of balance between them, and a reflection of the higher Kether sphere.

And still the pressure leads to change, bringing into being other states – Netzach, Hod and Yesod. With the latter, we approach the physical. With the final sphere, Malkuth, we reach it.

I don't know how much sense any of this has made to you. Possibly you would prefer the old Gnostic notion of God creating the physical world via a series of emanations. It is not strictly true, but then my talk of spheres and forces is not strictly true either. All we have to go on are symbols of reality.

The spheres, from Kether down to Malkuth, make up the Tree of Life. There is an inverse Tree as well, but Qabalists prefer not to talk of it. This inverse Tree represents Chaos. Its spheres are the states of existence of the Qlipoth, the Lords of Chaos, the Demons of the Pit. They are nasty forces to handle.

Where does humanity figure in this scheme of things? Our first observable fact is that Man is a part of the physical universe. Its laws are his laws. Since the states of the Tree are inherent in all matter, they are inherent in Man. Where Man differs from most things is that he may become aware of them.

As the innermost core of the universe is Kether, so the innermost core of Man is the Kether spark. He is, so to speak, a chip off the cosmic block.

'And God said, Let us make man in our image, after our likeness . . .'

There can be no question of greater or lesser being here. A fire may throw off a spark, but the spark has exactly the same essence of the fire. To produce mankind, billions of divine sparks were thrown off from the central flame. Each one, in the process of manifestation, became overlaid with the microcosmic equivalent of the Tree's spheres. The final overlay was the physical body.

There is, so to speak, a divine plan for humanity. It is embodied in the Tree. But somewhere something went askew.

'Therefore the Lord God sent him forth from the garden of Eden, to till the ground from whence he was taken.'

To the Qabalist who understands these things, there is only one real purpose – to correct, so far as he is able, the deviation in the Divine Plan. He begins the job by correcting, again so far as he is able, the deviation in his own Tree.

No one pretends the job is easy.

'So he drove out the man; and he placed at the east of the garden of Eden Cherubims, and a flaming sword which turned every way, to keep the way of the tree of life.'

The Biblical quotations are not inserted as a subtle appeal to the authority of Holy Writ. I used them in the faint hope of bringing an air of familiarity into a series of very obscure and unfamiliar concepts.

If you have ever taken the trouble to compare the ancient creation myths, Hebrew and otherwise, with modern scientific theories about the origin of the universe, you will have become aware of a very strange thing: the two are just the same. There are, of course, differences in terminology, but the basic ideas are identical. This is not to say, as some people have tried to, that the ancients were equipped with advanced scientific knowledge. It is to say that the human mind works essentially the same way whether the date is A.D. 2000 or 2000 B.C.

And in order to understand the Qabalah, your mind has to be shifted out of those familiar grooves. The technique necessary to accomplish this is meditation.

Find a good book on the Qabalah. (I can recommend Dion Fortune's *The Mystical Qabalah* or Gareth Knight's *Practical Guide to Qabalistic Symbolism.*) Read it chapter by chapter and meditate regularly on each one as you go. This is, I'm sorry to say, the only way. You will find it a long road but a worthwhile one. As you tread it, eventually you will come to realize something very comforting. Ultimately the angels are on the winning side. And this is not because they are good, or because they are strong. It is simply an inevitable aspect of the cosmic situation. Once you realize that, you can safely practise High Magic.

# PART TWO – HIGH MAGIC

## CHAPTER NINE

## ALIEN DIMENSIONS

You are in a partitioned room, equipped with a juke-box. The machine is specially set to play a random selection of records, twenty-four hours a day, at maximum volume. You have been told there is another juke-box on the far side of the partition. But since you cannot see through the partition and it resists all attempts at breaking down, you have never examined this second machine. Furthermore, the second machine has been set at minimum volume, so you cannot even hear if it is playing because of the noise from your own juke-box.

For a variety of reasons, you decide to investigate the nature of the second juke-box. Your first obvious move is to switch off your own. But once you try, you find that switching off presents such enormous difficulties that you are likely to settle for turning your own machine down to the lowest possible volume.

By doing so, you are in a position to learn something about the music played beyond the partition. Yet with all your efforts, the situation is far from ideal. Until you have attuned your ear through continual practice, you will not be able to tell whether the faint sounds you hear actually originate from the other side of the partition, or come, in fact, from the muted juke-box in your own half of the room.

This situation is very similar to the situation you find yourself in when first you try to make contact with the Inner Planes.

The occultist teaches that the Inner Planes are alien dimensions lying *on the other side of your mind*. It is not an easy idea to grasp fully. Can words like 'other side' have any meaning in this context? And even if there is an 'other side', how can you be sure the Inner Planes lie there and are not simply aspects of the mind itself? You are back to your partitioned room. Is there really another juke-box on the other side? Is there really an 'other side' to the partition at all?

What makes the problem even more troublesome is that you

cannot reach these alien dimensions directly. The partition cannot be broken down, any more than fire can mix with water. The best you can hope for is indirect knowledge – the faint strains of music from the second juke-box.

And even this indirect knowledge must be gained in the most suspect manner possible. For the occultist insists that the key to the Inner Places is . . . pure imagination.

Imagination is one of the most curious functions of the human mind, and one of the least appreciated. When a child day-dreams, he is advised sharply to come down to earth. When a man sees a ghost, he is told it is 'just imagination' as if this totally negated any value in his experience. Hallucinations are treated with little more than passing reference to their content. Walter Mitty is a figure of fun, or pity.

Yet side by side with this pervasive attitude lies the fact that every worthwhile achievement of the human race springs out of this single curious function. Works of art, from paintings to novels to symphonies, begin in the imagination. So do inventions. So do the technological applications of physical laws. The shape of your house began as a vision in the mind of an architect. The cut of your clothes stemmed from a designer's vision.

Imagination towers like a colossus even over the achievements of science. Einstein's Theory of Relativity was, initially, a gigantic leap of the imagination. The mathematical work came later. Darwin used imagination to help him synthesize his observations into an overall concept of evolution. Newton's apple stimulated the same faculty.

If you examine, let's say, a painting from the occult viewpoint, an interesting sequence emerges. The artist starts with nothing other than the tools of his trade – paints, brushes and an empty canvas. Then he visualizes the picture he wants to paint, calling its various elements before his inner eye. Whether he imagines the picture in its totality before he begins, or builds it up, so to speak, as he goes along, does not matter. In every case, he evokes the picture first as an act of imagination. *And this is his only creative act.*

What so many people think of as the act of creation – the brushwork on the canvas – is no more than the translation into

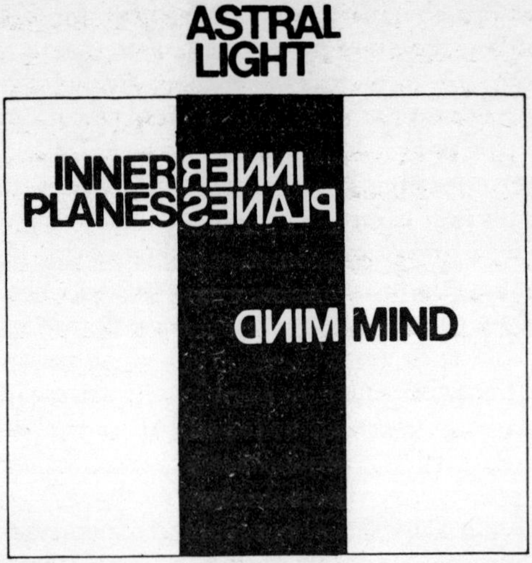


fig 5

physical terms of the mental pictures. At this stage what the artist uses is skill, not creativity. The occultist sees this as the 'earthing' of a creative act which took place on another plane.

This total sequence is worth stressing, for it is a typically magical sequence. Beginning with nothing, we evoke certain stresses on another plane. These are then earthed through skill, training and knowledge. And the result is a change on the physical plane. Virtually every magical operation proceeds in exactly the same way. Small wonder poets and artists take so easily to magic.

Once you begin to examine these facts, the occultist's use of the imagination as a means of contact with the Inner Planes ceases to be quite so ridiculous as it may have appeared at first. But it is still an operation plagued by enormous difficulties.

Following a centuries-old tradition, occultists refer to the realm of the imagination as the Astral Plane, or sometimes the Astral Light. For the purpose of this discussion, you can think of it as a borderland, touching on the mind to one side and on the Inner Planes to the other. In itself, this borderland area is formless, but it has the curious property of taking on any form impressed upon it, in other words of giving forces shape. It is, essentially, a plastic medium.

Before this becomes too obscure, we had better hark back to the artist. When he first began his act of creativity, there was nothing. His inner eye stared out on the formless billows of the Astral Light. His imagination presented him with a blank screen, matching the blank canvas in his studio. But he desired a picture. He had the will to create one and the inexplicable ability to evoke its form in his imagination. In other words, the forces of his mind created stresses in the Astral Light which, by its nature, translated them into form, the form of the required picture.

Having realized the nature of the Astral Light, you can quickly appreciate the problems of using it as a mirror of the Inner Planes. The forces of the Inner Planes may influence it, but so too do the forces of your own mind. Through every waking minute (and most of your sleeping hours) your thoughts, emotions and desires are impressing forms upon the Astral Light. You are creating continual turbulence. While these circumstances last, contacting the Inner Planes is as difficult as viewing a fish while stirring up a pool. If I may revert back to my earlier analogy, your juke-box is making so much noise that it drowns out all other sounds.

So the first step in contact involves getting your juke-box under control. Obtaining total control of your mind is roughly on a par with climbing Everest – only a very few can manage it. But unless you have previously undertaken training, it is almost certain that you can develop greater control of your mind than you have now. Like everything else, it is a matter of training and practice.

Fortunately, if you have been playing with Low Magic – particularly the five-pound note trick – you will already have had training and practice in the most important essentials: relaxation and visualization.

In Low Magic, relaxation was advocated primarily to break down the tension barrier which tends to block any free flow of spiritual energies. Now, the same technique is put to use for a slightly different purpose – cutting down distractions.

This approach lies very close to the theory of Hatha Yoga. In the West, Hatha Yoga (usually in a modified form) is presented as a physical fitness programme, a sort of pseudo-mystical substitution for morning press-ups or a run around the block. But in the East, where the various Yogas were developed, Hatha Yoga has a much more far-reaching purpose.

The aspirant has one goal in mind – conscious union with the Godhead. To prepare himself for this ecstatic experience, he must first make sure his body will not distract him. It is a very realistic approach to assume that no one thinks divine thoughts with a stomach ache.

Consequently, the yogi uses Hatha techniques to ensure perfect fitness and, even more important, perfect control of his body. Should the whisper of his breath disturb his meditations, he can still it. Should the pounding of his heart distract him, he can slow it to a murmur. These are, of course, extreme results of very lengthy application. But extreme or not, the principle underlying them remains constant.

I am not, bluntly, an advocate of Yoga. It is a fine system for the East, but my experience has been that Westerners applying the techniques without adequate supervision (and genuine gurus are as rare in the West as snowballs in Africa) are simply asking for trouble. But this does not deny that the thinking behind the Eastern techniques is sound. From Benares to Birmingham, it makes sense to cut down physical distractions while pursuing the eternal verities.

Fortunately, the remarkable degree of control developed by Hatha Yoga is unnecessary in the West, at least so far as Inner Plane contact is concerned. Properly applied, relaxation will do the trick just as well. If you refer back to Chapter Three, you will find the technique given in detail.

While deep relaxation is no cure-all, it will certainly help make a number of complaints more bearable. Furthermore, a relaxed body tends to have an altered pain threshold, with the result that aches and pains become a lot less troublesome.

Almost certainly, your biggest single problem will be maintaining the relaxed state. There is always a tendency for tension to creep in once your attention wanders. The only real answer is continual practice, until relaxation becomes a habit.

Continued relaxation is important. When distractions have been reduced to a minimum and Inner Plane contacts established, there is a strong likelihood of a force-flow along the lines of contact. Should the flow meet a sudden tension barrier, you will find yourself, to put it mildly, in an uncomfortable position. Worse still, the more successfully you have made contact, the more dangerous it is to erect the sudden barrier.

The dangers of the force-flow do not end with tension. This is a point I shall return to shortly in dealing fully with the necessary preparations for contact. Just now, I want to make absolutely sure you appreciate the mechanics of the astral operation involved in such contacts.

First, examine your situation.

I have suggested, in common with many other occult writers, that there is an alien dimension on the other side of your mind. You are interested enough to wish to explore this dimension, but appreciate that by its nature (and your own) you cannot simply pull on hiking boots and walk there. You are, to some extent, in the position of a submarine commander who wants to view the surface. Obviously he cannot simply stick his head out. Instead, he makes use of an ingenious arrangement of mirrors in a periscope. Through this instrument he can view the outside world usefully, if not directly. The limits of his vision are the limits of his instrument. The clarity of his vision depends entirely on how skilfully the instrument was constructed.

In viewing the Inner Planes, you are making use of the instrument of imagination. In other words, you hope to see the entities and forces of these alien dimensions reflected on this potent mental screen. Just as the submarine commander cannot keep his eye to the periscope if his attention is continually being drawn to trouble in the engine room, you have learned that you cannot keep your mental eye fixed on the Astral Light if you are continually distracted by the calls of the body. Consequently, you have decided to reduce these distractions to a workable minimum by the practice of relaxation.

But you have still to prepare the instrument, and preparation is far from easy. This is one of the main reasons why so very few occultists master the practice of High Magic, while literally thousands have some command of the system in its lower forms.

From this point on, through the preparation of the 'astral periscope' and beyond, there is one vitally important thing to remember. When you make an Inner Plane contact by these methods, the forms you see are astral forms, a translation by your imagination faculty of forces from the Beyond. The forces are potent, the forms impressive, but it is a fool's game accepting symbol for reality. The only justification for using an astral form of contact is the hope that it will eventually lead you to a direct experience of spiritual reality.

## CHAPTER TEN

# MEDITATION

Even if you have read less than a dozen books on the occult, chances are you have already noticed the great stress laid on the 'Mysteries', the 'Mystery Schools' of antiquity and their sublime system of initiation.

A number of bodies exist today laying claim to similar techniques and results as the ancient Mystery Schools. Many of these bodies peddle a greater or lesser degree of self-deception. A few of them are outright rackets. A very few have some genuine backing to their claims. But Schools in the final category are hard to find. They seldom, if ever, advertise. They make no attempts at missionary work. There is a current belief among their principals that when a pupil is ready, mysterious forces will lead him to the training he needs.

Even if you are lucky (or evolved) enough to find a genuine Mystery School of the present day, entrance is seldom easy. The barriers are not financial. Any occult School worthy of the name will give tuition free if the occasion warrants it. But no School worth its salt will take on a dilettante. To gain admission, you will work, and work hard, over a period of years. Often, to maintain your membership, you are required to work even harder. And the work itself is the most onerous you could imagine, for it is work on your own personality and character.

Aside from these well-hidden organizations, there is only one genuine system of initiation widely available to the European. It was devised by Sigmund Freud, whose interest in the Qabalah is seldom stressed in his biographies, and is called psychoanalysis. While psychoanalysis is widely available, it is not, unfortunately, freely available. Furthermore, it was devised not as a system of initiation, but as a therapy and is still generally used as such, despite impressive evidence of uselessness.

These factors represent distinct drawbacks of the system. It is pointless approaching a psychiatrist unless you have a great deal of hard cash to spend. This is no slur on the psychiatrist, merely an indication of the time and effort which must go into a complete analysis. And money isn't everything. Few competent (if, in my view, misguided) doctors will waste their time with a healthy patient. They will reserve analysis for the neurotic, who will benefit by it in every way, except relief of symptoms.

Fortunately the principles of psychoanalysis are much easier to come by. Freud left a mass of writings on his system and these have been enlarged and extended by hundreds of his followers. Nor is this psychiatric literature always difficult or obscure. Freud himself wrote with the flow of a novelist.

Any of you tempted to embark on the establishment of Inner Plane contact as suggested in later pages, would be well advised to gain a working knowledge of psychiatric literature before you begin. It will give you important insights into the workings of the mind and help you develop self-knowledge. A fund of self-knowledge, the richer the better, is vitally important to any astral investigation of the Inner Planes. A moment's thought will show you why.

Remember that you will see the Inner Planes reflected in the Astral Light. But that Light reflects your own hopes, desires and ambitions as well. You will, of course, do all you can to still your mind, but until you reach a very advanced stage, you will find total stillness virtually impossible to achieve. In the interim, therefore, it becomes important to differentiate between an Inner Plane reflection and a projection of your own unconscious mind. For this, the only tool you have is self-knowledge.

This is an area where, regrettably, many occultists come to grief. Unconscious projections can be both subtle and appealing. The mechanics of wish-fulfilment give you, by definition, what you have always wanted. The explosive results of occult interest without self-knowledge can be seen very clearly in certain areas of the United States, where new cult Messiahs spring up with truly alarming regularity.

Even if you do not drift into spectacular psychosis, there are a thousand lesser shades of self-deception. At best without self-knowledge, you run the risk of turning an important adventure into a series of illusions.

It is not enough to learn the jargon of psychiatry – you must put it into practice. is not to say you should become another of the armchair psychologists so prevalent nowadays. It is to suggest that, having read the books, you should attempt to understand the underlying principles and put them to work in evaluating your own impulses and reactions.

Along with psychiatric theory, there are a number of other valuable tools for the development of self-knowledge. Possibly the foremost amongst them is meditation.

For some reason, meditation has become cloaked in mystery. There must be hundreds of books on the market, promising to reveal its 'secrets'. Yet the most difficult thing about meditation is the initial decision to try it.

Admittedly, depth meditation is something of an art. But it is an art you will not learn by reading books. The only way to develop it is to practise it. And the only way to practise it is to sit right down and start. Meditation simply means thinking consistently about a given subject. You follow up the train of thought that arises, turning the subject over and over in your mind, examining it from various angles.

Ideally, you should set aside a given time each day for meditation. Here again, a habit is easily established, and it is a good one. But don't be too ambitious. Oriental adepts may spend days and years in constant meditation. You should limit yourself to fifteen or twenty minutes, at least in the early stages.

Make sure you won't be disturbed. Lock the door of your room, if necessary. Like so many occult exercises, early morning is best, if for no other reason than that you are less likely to be disturbed. And, again as in many other occult exercises, relaxation is a necessary preliminary.

Sit in a straight chair and make yourself comfortable with a footstool. There is always the possibility of falling asleep, hence the straight chair which will ensure you only stay asleep the short time it takes you to fall on the floor.

Now go through the relaxation process. As I've mentioned elsewhere, there is a distinct relationship between a relaxed body and a relaxed mind. Without a relaxed mind, you won't get far in meditation.

Now start to think about your chosen subject. Since you are seeking self-knowledge, it would be as well to pick something relevant, your emotional reactions for instance, or the make-up of your personality.

At first, even with such a fascinating subject as yourself, your mind will wander. Don't let this worry you. It is a perfectly common occurrence. Make a note of any breaks in concentration, then forget them. As time goes on and you gain proficiency, you will find the breaks becoming fewer and fewer.

Constant meditation has the effect of wearing down the barrier between your conscious and unconscious mind. Soon you will find ideas and information arising from the deeper strata.

Another excellent tool for carving knowledge of your inner self is systematic tabulation. In its simplest form, this simply means making two lists – one taking in your good points, the other your bad points. The trick is to work on the lists until you can't think of another single item to put down . . . then convince yourself you're really only starting.

A more sophisticated – and considerably more useful – variation of this basic principle is an elemental breakdown.

As you probably know, the ancients subdivided matter into four basic elements – Earth, Air, Fire and Water – ruled over by a subtle fifth, Ether or Spirit. With the development of modern chemistry, the elements of matter went out of fashion, but the subdivision holds remarkably good when applied to human psychology.

Rule a page into five and head each column with an element name. Then try to fit each of your characteristics into the relevant column. If, for instance, you suffer from outbursts of temper, this should obviously be noted under Fire. Laziness would fit well under Earth. Charitable acts (unless prompted by social pressures or a desire to save income tax) should be listed under Ether. And so on.

The particular benefit of the elemental breakdown is that you can soon see at a glance where any imbalance lies. If you've made two dozen entries under 'Air' and one each under the remaining headlines, then obviously something is very wrong with your inner make-up. Not only that, but you know the area of over-emphasis. In these circumstances, you can often do something to correct the balance. As a matter of passing interest, a number of occultists recommend meditation on each of the elements in strict rotation as a means of achieving inner balance. The idea is excellent, provided you realize that information obtained in meditation must at some stage be translated into action.

In your search for self-knowledge, it is a useful approach to find out what friends and acquaintances think of you. It may take a certain amount of nerve to ask and a good deal of time to persuade them to tell the truth, but the results are usually worth the effort.

The outsider will make no allowance for your faults, while you will almost certainly fail to notice them at all. This single difference is vital to an honest evaluation.

Dream analysis can be another interesting approach. Catch your dreams by keeping a notebook and pencil at your bedside and writing down the details the second you wake up. (Leave it even for a minute and the dream evaporates.) During your analysis of dream content, you can throw away every popular book on the 'meaning' of dreams you have ever purchased. And, oddly enough, you can forget most of the tomes on psychological symbolism as well. Your dream is your own. No one can interpret it but yourself.

Certainly your dream will be packed with symbols. But the important thing is what those symbols mean to *you.* A Freudian may put up convincing arguments that a snake symbolizes the penis. But to you it could symbolize extreme amusement because you once watched a snake eat your grandfather's hat. So look for the *personal* symbolism in your dreams and evaluate them accordingly.

Armed with self-knowledge and the trained ability to relax at will, your other great preliminary essential to Inner Plane contact is concentration.

Like the ability to visualize, which you have developed to some degree during your experiments with Low Magic, concentration is a matter of practice. If you have followed the path of meditation in your search for self-knowledge, you will, as a sideline, have developed a fair degree of concentration as well. But there is concentration and concentration. Occultists and psychologists recognize two main types, voluntary and involuntary. Should you be unfortunate enough to find your foot on fire at this moment, it is unlikely you will continue to pay much attention to this book. Instead, your mind will be entirely concentrated on the pain you experience. This is *involuntary* concentration, with not a great deal you can do about it.

Involuntary concentration can arise in much more pleasant circumstances. When something interests you, your attention is drawn towards it. Consequently, it is easier for most people to concentrate on a sex scene in a book by Harold Robbins that on an article about cybernetics in the *Encyclopedia Britannica.* You will appreciate involuntary concentration needs no development. It simply follows naturally on interest.

Voluntary concentration arises from a different set of circumstances. Here you make a decision to concentrate on something which may run contrary to your natural interests. Your concentration is then held on the subject by an act of will. This is obviously a good deal less easy than involuntary concentration and the chances are you won't do it very well. Once again, the answer is practice, for voluntary concentration, often of a high degree, will certainly be necessary in most High Magic workings.

Although your meditation practice will have helped, this type of exercise cannot do the job completely. This is because in meditation, you are concentrating on a chain of associated ideas as you spin out your train of thought. In other words, you have the help of novelty. Some High workings require a much more static focus for your concentration and it is as well to prepare for it.

In the next chapter, I will outline some exercises which will help here. But though, diligently performed, they develop voluntary concentration, and a degree of visualization, this is not their primary purpose. Their primary purpose is to make sure your psyche can stand up to the force of spiritual contact.

## CHAPTER ELEVEN

# RITUAL WORKINGS

Later, you will learn what occult ritual is all about. In the interim, I want to set out a ritual for you to practise.

This operation was developed, so far as I know, by the Order of the Golden Dawn and has passed into widespread use amongst Western occult fraternities. It is far from secret. There must be half a dozen books before me as I write which give both inner and outer workings.

The ritual – the Lesser Banishing Ritual of the Pentagram – is normally used to prepare a room for subsequent ceremonial. Properly carried out, it affects the atmosphere of a place and performs essentially the same job on the astral level as disinfectant on the physical.

But this widely published ritual has a lesser-known variation and a lesser-known use. It can, in fact, refine the psyche of the operator.

Since the ritual is so widely available in published form, I will keep the outline description as brief as possible.

### Outer Working

Face east. Raise right hand above head, bring down to forehead, say, 'Ateh'.

Bring hand down to touch chest, say 'Malkuth'.

Touch right shoulder, say, 'Ve Geburah'.

Touch left shoulder, say, 'Ve Gedulah'.

Clasp hands together on breast, say, 'Le olahim, amen'.

(This sequence is known as the Qabalistic Cross.)

With fingers of right hand pointing, draw pentagram in air, beginning with hand at left hip. Stab figure through centre and vibrate name *Yoh-he-vav-he.*

Move to south, repeat and vibrate *Adonai.*

Move to west, repeat and vibrate, *Eh-he-yeh.*

Move to north, repeat and vibrate, *Ag-el-ah.*

Return to east, stretch out arms, say, 'Before me Raphael. Behind me Gabriel. On my right hand Michael. On my left hand Uriel. About me flame the pentagrams. Behind me shines the six-rayed star.'

Repeat Qabalistic Cross.

**Inner Working**

As you bring your hand down, visualize a shaft of white light descending from the Kether centre above the crown of your head down to your feet.

As the hand is brought from right shoulder to left, visualize a shaft of white light following it through your body.

As the hands are clasped on the breast, visualize a steady white flame between them.

As you draw each pentagram, visualize its component lines as burning with a bluish-white flame.

As you stab the centre and move on to each of the cardinal points, visualize a line of this blue-white flame emerging from your fingertips and thus eventually drawing a complete circle around you.

As the names of the archangels are pronounced, visualize as follows:

Raphael – Robed in yellow, hair moving in the wind. Sensation of cooling breeze from that quarter.

Gabriel – Robed in blue, with stream or sea at feet.

Michael – Robed in red, standing on parched earth or desert. Radiates heat.

Uriel – Robed in citrine, olive, russet and black (overall impression is simply a dark robe). Stands in rich wheatfield.

Such, briefly, is the basic working. Unless you happen already to be familiar with it, it would be no bad thing to practise the ritual as given for a time to get the feel of it. When it is fluid and familiar, move on to the modification I will give you and use it daily for a minimum of two months.

The first step towards the modification – and the most important step – is to recognize what you intend the ritual to do. This you will achieve by meditation on the following proposition.

Your mind is not *in* your body. Rather, your body is *within* your mind. You move, ultimately, in a sea of consciousness.

While a magical operation (including the Pentagram Ritual) may be designed to affect the outer world, it can only do so by first acting on the inner. If you accept that the ritual will, in a manner of speaking, 'disinfect' the environment, you must also accept that it does so by first 'disinfecting' a portion of all of your psyche. Continual use of the ritual, with intent, will produce a permanent 'cleansing' of the psyche.

Meditation will convince you of the essential logic of this proposition, thus enabling you to 'solidify' your intent on using the ritual. But as you do, there are slight technical modifications to carry out.

In the most usual form of the ritual, the pentagrams remain static. That is, they are drawn in place and stay there as cardinal guardians of an enclosed circle. When using the ritual for (if the health-salt people will forgive me) 'inner cleanliness', the pentagrams are visualized as moving. That is, they are drawn originally close to the body and seen in the mind's eye as swimming outwards, clearing a way as they go.

The second, and final, modification is not, strictly speaking, a modification at all, but an addition. You should, by this stage, be reasonably well aware of your major faults. On using the ritual, visualize these faults *in personified form* and place them beyond the circle enclosed by the ritual. See them wither and die there for lack of nourishment.

Once your visualization abilities are developed, none of this should prove very difficult, except perhaps the personification of faults, which requires a certain creative faculty. If personification does not come easily to you, picture the scene in your life when the particular fault last manifested, and place that scene beyond the circle.

As in almost every other occult exercise, regularity of practice is important. Perform the ritual each day and over the weeks you will begin to feel a gradual benefit.

This following exercise is a development of an exercise you have already learned. As such, it is an example of how vague the dividing line is between Low and High magic. At many points, the two blend and only the final outcome shows where a particular exercise, ritual or operation belongs.

Like the Pentagram Ritual, the Fountain Exercise should be practised daily for a period of at least two months before an Inner Plane contact is attempted.

(It occurs to me at this point that a few of my fellow occultists may consider my approach ultra-cautious. So it is. But I would prefer to help a few students with safety than to open the system to the greater numbers who lack perseverance and take grave risks in the process.)

The Fountain Exercise is as follows.

Relax consciously and begin the 2/4 breathing sequence.

Activate the Middle Pillar.

Circulate the Kether force as you were taught in Chapter Four.

When you have completed half a dozen circuits of the force (i.e. six each circling to the side and to the front) throw your attention to the Malkuth sphere at your feet. Imagine energy from that sphere rising up the Middle Pillar until it reaches the Kether sphere above your head. Visualize this on a single inbreath to the count of four.

Now, to the count of two, hold this energy in quivering suspension above your head. At the same time, hold your breath.

Then, on a 4-count outbreath, visualize the energy pouring all over you in a waterfall of light. The effect is something similar to a Roman Candle firework, except that in your visualization, only white light is used.

This completes one fountain sequence. Before beginning another, you should rest for a complete breathing sequence. Consequently you will, without visualizing, hold your breath out, to the count of two; breathe in to the count of four; hold your breath in for a count of two; and breathe out to a count of four.

As you are holding your breath out for the next count of two, again bring your attention to the Malkuth centre, and repeat the fountain sequence on the inbreath.

The Fountain Exercise should be repeated at least six times in all, with the 'rest' sequence between each one.

An interesting indication that you are performing the exercise properly is that the Middle Pillar centres seem to 'click on' as the light is drawn upwards through them. The sensation is a difficult one to describe, but once you feel it, you will not mistake it.

The Fountain Exercise is a safe sequence which could scarcely be overdone if you tried. But there is one slight danger attached to it. This is the danger of forgetting where the power came from in the first place. Your prime contact with the cosmic source is, of course, the Kether centre above your head. It is through this sphere that all energy comes in the first instance, feeding the remaining spheres with a force which they adapt and transform to the specific psycho-physical needs.

To lose sight of this fact is to run the risk of setting in motion adverse currents in the aura. Should this occur, there is too the slight, but real, danger of the premature arousal of the Kundalini force – a shattering experience for the unprepared.

A third, quite useful exercise to prepare you for Inner Plane contact is 'pore breathing'. A fact Ian Fleming helped to make famous is that pores *do* breathe. Coat an attractive young woman with gold paint, thus blocking each pore, and she will fairly quickly die. But this is not exactly what occultists mean. Once again, the exercise is one of visualization.

Relax systematically and begin a 2/4 breathing sequence. When the rhythm is established, fix your awareness on the fact that air – and energy – is flowing in through your nose into your lungs. Realize that your body is taking oxygen and energy from this inflow, replacing it with the waste product of carbon dioxide. Realize too that as you breathe out, this waste product is carried out and away from your body.

Now take the whole thing a step further. Imagine that instead of breathing in only through your nose, you are breathing in through every pore in your body. This vast sea of light and energy is being drawn in through every single pore.

Properly done (and the exercise is a remarkably easy one) pore breathing produces a curious and quite unmistakable sensation somewhere between a tingle and an energy upsurge.

Breathing in 'through the pores' is, of course, only the first step of the exercise. As you hold your breath on the two-count, visualize the light as filling your entire body and being absorbed by it.

Then, as you breathe out to the count of four, visualize your unwanted psychic qualities flowing out through your pores along with the waste of the body.

(Although it has not strict relevance to Inner Plane contact, pore breathing can sometimes work wonders for physical ailments in specific categories. The trick is to breathe through a certain area, not always the seat of the pain, thus increasing the supply of psychic energy to that part. The technique does not produce quick cures, but it is often very effective in the long term.)

Pore breathing is like every other breathing exercise, excellent therapy so long as it is not overdone. More than any other, this occult technique is like salt on your stew – just because a little is fine doesn't mean a lot will be better.

So keep your pore breathing experiments short in the early stages. Start with three minutes a day for the first week, gradually working up to a maximum of fifteen.

If you practise the Pentagram Ritual in conjunction with the Fountain Exercise, pore breathing is not strictly necessary to prepare you for the Inner Contacts. But if circumstances allow, there is no harm in combining the three. In any case, continue these exercises for at least two months before attempting the contact technique outlined in the next chapter.

## CHAPTER TWELVE

# SEARCHING FOR MIRACLES

Any man who interests himself in the occult is a bit of a romantic, a bit of a fool. Like Ouspensky, he tends to travel in search of the miraculous and unless he is very lucky he sometimes finds it. He will also find, without much doubt, the phoney article. The phoney article can be quite fascinating in its own way, for often it is not entirely phoney; or perhaps it is genuine, but misrepresented, like E.P.N.S. over platinum.

I walked, with Helen and Johanna, up endless narrow wooden stairs in search of the miraculous. The doorway we entered had been mean and dingy, next to a greengrocer's shop. The stairs themselves were dirty, so that dust rose as we walked and caught in our throats. Somewhere near the top, we heard a perfectly indescribable sound. We followed it to its source and found ourselves in the seance room. The sound came from cagebirds, perhaps as many as fifty of them, along the walls.

The room was large, but a good third of it had been filled with junk. Old oil paintings and dusty lithographs of stags at bay were stacked against heavy antique tables, china dogs and chamber-pots. On one wall was a little darkroom light. At the other end of the room were two dozen Sunday-go-to-Meeting wooden chairs, monsters of discomfort, set out in rows. A lectern faced them and on it a huge, open Bible, ponderous and dignified as the Book of Life.

Each Saturday evening, while voluptuaries watched television or huddled in a cinema, this room was the site of contacts with the Dead – or so Johanna told me.

The congregation, when it had finished drifting in, turned out to be small, odd and almost entirely feminine. Apart from myself and the medium, there was only one other man in the place, and he looked distinctly uncomfortable.

The women seemed to fall broadly into two categories. There were the plump poor, dressed up in a Sunday best that might have been left over from the reign of Queen Victoria. And there were the thin neurotics, very intense and very pale as if they spent too much time in surroundings like this.

When the medium arrived, he shattered all illusions. There was neither power nor personality about him. He was a small man, tiny almost, about fifty years old and thin. He looked hopeless. There was a greyness about him as if dust had collected in the lines of his face. His suit was a nondescript green, unpressed and stained. His fingernails were enormously long, like those of Chinese mandarin, and quite filthy.

He was also lazy. The weekly seances were his livelihood. He eked out a living from the meagre donations of these curious, impoverished women and the occasional casual caller like myself. But he disliked giving value for money. He was a medium who preferred not to function.

Johanna told me he had been caught cheating at least once. Someone had switched on the light during a trumpet seance and found him on hands and knees waving the instrument about in the air. But she felt his talent was genuine despite the fraud.

The proceedings started with the singing of a hymn. It was unaccompanied and tuneless and gave the whole meeting the feeling of a small town revival. Then our medium read a piece from the Bible, something suitably disturbing about the 'Last Days' and suitably spiritualistic about 'speaking with tongues'. And then the lights went off, except for the little red darkroom light at the far end, and we waited.

We waited not for our little thin medium, who preferred to conserve his energies, but for the developing mediums (media?) in the congregation. We did not have long to wait. A woman with cherries on her hat and eyes that flashed like a cat's in the half light, rose to deliver messages in a pleasant, vibrant voice.

'I have a message from Mary . . .'

'That's my mother!' (Excitedly.)

'She says she is the mother of someone present here tonight . . .'

'It's her! It's her!'

It was all perfectly wonderful and perfectly phoney. Not, of course, a con game (for con games are really remarkably hard to find in Spiritualism) but a mass of deception, mutual and self, as people without much drama in their lives got together in a conspiracy to produce some.

In this atmosphere oddities occasionally occurred. The human mind is a curious thing and the group mind is even odder. In the dim light with emotions roused, strange things happened. A stirring subconscious might stretch out telekinetic tendrils to produce a poltergeist or two. An hysterical woman might, quite unconsciously, steal information from another mind.

Such things happen daily among Spiritualists. They have nothing to do with post mortem communication (although confusion between the two is rife amongst the faithful) but may someday prove a mine of interest to the parapsychologists. They are the platinum beneath the E.P.N.S.

Very many years later, still searching for the miraculous, I found myself alone in London. It was a quiet end of the city, an avenue with trees where you could actually forget you stood upon a plain of concrete that stretched for miles without a break whichever way you turned.

My taxi-driver had looked up at the houses, sucked in breath and opined that the nobs lived here. But he was only trying out applied psychology in the hope of a bigger tip. Anyone with half an eye could see the district was in decline. The nobs had once lived here certainly, but not any more. Those who remained were strictly members of the stranded gentry.

I walked through a little garden overgrown with shrubs. The greenery was London green, as if soot had managed to discolour the living plants. I rang the bell.

It was as if I had been swept back through the years. The woman who opened the door would have dropped into that phoney seance without creating a ripple on the surface. She was, by physical type, one of the fat poor. But she was completely silent, which was totally out of character for the type.

I went to a little ante-room where I prepared myself with meditation for some fifteen or twenty minutes. Then I was escorted down a flight of stairs to a very different sort of seance. The room was a Lodge Room, constructed and prepared by ritualists. It was furnished with, among other things, the traditional altar and pillars. Lodge officers, mediating archetypal figures, stood, or sat, at the cardinal points. There was incense and candlelight.

There was also, it occurs to me now, the utter professionalism – no other word can describe it – of a group that knows what it is doing.

The room had been prepared by ritual, almost certainly a variation of the Pentagram Ritual given earlier. It had, I presume, been used time and again for evocation. The effect of that room was staggering.

If you have ever walked any distance on a frosty winter's day before pushing open a door into a centrally-heated building, you will know what I mean by a wall of air. There was a wall of air at the doorway of the Lodge Room. But its essence was not heat but something else, something that could be sensed perfectly (and, it seemed, at a physical level) by the nerve endings beneath the skin of the face. Houses have 'atmosphere', a welcoming feeling or a rejection, an aura of warmth or chill. This was atmosphere solidified, an atmosphere that literally 'hits you in the face'.

There were no fireworks in the working that followed, no trances or weird shadows in the incense smoke – just results and an atmosphere pregnant with power.

The essential difference between these two groups was that the second I described had formed a link with the Inner Planes and was drawing power from the other side of the collective mind. The first group had power too, for it produced occasional phenomena. But it was power drawn only from the subconscious and to that extent was phoney where the operation of High Magic is concerned.

Inner Plane contacts are most often made within a group setting. The trick is easier that way. But links may be forged by individuals, if they go about it the right way.

There are, in fact, a number of methods. They produce different kinds of contact, although all originate in essentially the same area. It is as if you had three friends in New York. One owned a telex machine, one a telephone, while the third, impoverished or just sensible, owned neither. You can make contact with all three in different ways. A telex contact is not a telephone contact is not a letter contact. Yet your friends all live in New York.

The Qabalist would, for instance, embark on Inner Plane contacts through treading the Paths of the Tree of Life. Unfortunately, to be undertaken properly, this technique requires considerable training in Qabalistic symbolism, which in turn requires a particular type of mind and interest. It is also true to say that while Path working may be a solitary affair, it is always far more successful if undertaken by a group. I have no quarrel with group work when undertaken for a specific purpose, but many groups become a way of life. This to my mind breeds a greater or lesser exclusiveness, a feeling of 'us' and 'them' that can be the death of spiritual development in its higher aspects.

The technique outlined in this chapter is not a Path working, but it arose out of a Path working. This is by no means unusual, as you will realize once you appreciate that any contact must be two-sided. You can only phone your friend in New York if he is willing to take the call.

Inner Plane entities will, as a general principle, 'take calls' from those of us who have gone beyond the playing stage. The form of contact is not a party game; and if it is approached in a party atmosphere, the lines of communication simply break down, leaving you at best with nothing and at worst with an obsessive fascination for the glittering nonsense sometimes produced through toying with the astral.

From time to time when a contact is made, those on the other side will suggest fresh methods and techniques of putting through a call. Sometimes these suggestions involve the reopening of old channels; sometimes the formation of new ones. In the present case, there is a little of both aspects.

By the time you come to begin this exercise, you will, or should, already have established a regular routine of occult exercises. Devote the time taken up by this routine to the establishment of your own Inner Plane contact. From this point until the contact is firmly established, *abandon all exercises other than those given.*

Your first task is the preparation of the place of working. This simply means the establishment of a suitable astral environment for contact to take place. Remember that the Astral Plane is fluid and you require a place of relative stability – a place to stand, as Archimedes said.

Semi-permanent edifices can be established on the astral only with a lot of hard work and repetition. This is why the reopening of old channels is often suggested: much of the hard work has already been done, the foundation is there and what is wanted, so to speak, is a cleaning out, a buttress on the walls and a fresh lick of paint.

Your astral place of working falls to some extent into this category. When the original place of contact was formed is a matter for speculation, but such speculation as has taken place suggests an ancient line with Nordic associations. Those interested in tying the matter down further may conduct their own experiments when contact is made.

There follows a description. Read it through, over and over, until you are perfectly familiar with it.

'You stand outside the walls of the city. They are high, grey walls, towering up out of a cold and barren landscape. There is a tremendous aura of endurance about these walls, a lasting strength.

'Before you are the twin gates of the city. These are wood, inlaid with brass and iron. They are massive gates and on your right, high above you, is the guard, helmeted, armed only with a spear, standing at his post on the walls of the city.

'There is a path twisting through the wasteland behind you; and you know that, in a way, you have trodden this path to reach the city.

'The gates swing open and you pass through. Immediately, in contrast to the cold and rather dreary wasteland, you are in bright sunlight. The avenues of the city are broad and clean, the houses high and built to a faintly Medieval architecture.

'And everywhere there are canals, sparkling silver waterways that wander through the city, intermingling with the avenues so that on every side, it seems, you are surrounded by bridges.

'These bridges are the most striking feature of the city, so that you will quickly come to think of it as the City of Bridges.

'Quickly, you will find your way on to the central avenue, a broad, straight thoroughfare boring its way to the very heart of the city. There are a few people about, golden-haired men and women strolling without haste. You pay them no attention, nor they you.

'As you walk, you feel, in a curious way, a growing familiarity with this place. You recognize that you know it; and will grow to know it with even deeper insight in the days ahead.

'And the city, in turn, will recognize you. You will feel its atmosphere welcoming, lifting you a little higher, a little straighter. Your body will feel just a little lighter as you walk within the city walls.

'Now you are nearing the end of your journey for the avenue widens into a vast courtyard. And before you, in the courtyard, is the tallest building you have yet seen. You have reached the Central Temple of the City of Bridges . . .'

Your inner journey is far from finished, but there is a natural break here. Having familiarized yourself with the description so far, begin to 'live it' in the following manner.

Sit in your chair and go through the conscious relaxation process. Perform the Fountain Exercise. Both of these are important preliminaries at this stage and absolutely vital when you go on to complete the exercise.

Making sure that no tension has crept back in, begin to visualize the journey from the gates of the city to the central temple, *as if you were actually undertaking it.* Build up the pictures as strongly as you are able, filling in as much detail as possible. The more you can make this picture 'live', the greater are your chances of successful contact with the Inner Planes.

Perform this exercise daily for at least two weeks, and preferably four, before you move on to its second stage, where you will establish the actual astral place of working.

## CHAPTER THIRTEEN

# A TEMPLE IN THE MIND

Virtually everything so far given, even your astral journey through the City of Bridges, has been preparation for what is to come now. For now you will continue your journey into the Central Temple itself; and it is here, when the time is ripe, that your contact will be made.

When you have practised the initial journey for the time specified, continue thus.

'As you watch, you can feel the aura of the temple pulling you towards it. You walk to the broad, white steps and begin to mount them towards a door set between tall, white, marble pillars. Like the gate of the city, this door is wood, inlaid with brass; but it has a newer, lighter appearance. As you mount the steps, it swings open.

'You pass through into a vast, domed hall of white marble. Colonnades of slender pillars run to your right and left. High above you, a window in the central dome allows a shaft of golden sunlight to pour through and strike the central altar.

'This altar, set as high as your waist on the marble floor, is draped in white, without ornament. Lying diagonally across it, with the handle towards you, is a broadsword. Behind the sword is a lighted lamp and beside that a dagger and chalice.

'Beyond the altar, in the east, are two thick pillars, towering to the roof: one black, the other silver. Between them, inlaid in the marble floor, is a circle with around its edge representations of the zodiacal signs.

'Nothing more stands in the temple, save a white marble throne in the east, beyond the pillars.

'You walk forward, moving to the left of the altar and beyond it, approaching the pillars and eventually taking your stand between them, facing west, your feet in the centre of the zodiac circle. You wait.

'You are now in the symbolic place of balance. Your body forms the Middle Pillar between those great pillars on either side of you. It is only from this spot that you may safely handle the cosmic spiritual forces. But the placing is symbolic. Meditate upon this.

'And wait . . .'

From this point on, there is very little to do *except* wait. You have gone as far as possible in the conscious preparation of the place. From this point on, the action must come from the other side: your friend in New York must decide to pick up the receiver.

Rest assured that on your first attempts, nothing more is likely to happen. But do not grow discouraged. Each time you visualize the sequence, you are establishing the environment more and more firmly in the Astral Plane.

You will find, as the weeks, and possibly months, go by, that your vision becomes clearer, more realistic, sharper in detail, fuller in depth. All these things, this increasing solidity, bring the moment of contact nearer.

What happens when contact occurs? In a way I can tell you; and in a way I cannot. When you ring your friend in New York, I can tell you approximately how you will be holding your phone, describe the dialling tone or the likely comments of the trans-Atlantic operator. But I cannot tell you what your friend will say, or what emotions you will feel at the news, or what action you may feel impelled to take because of it.

When you have built up the place of working sufficiently well and your contact on the other side of your mind closes the circuit, you will first feel an energizing sensation as you stand between the pillars. Exactly how you will experience this is difficult to say; but the sensation will be there. Possibly the feeling will be accompanied by some such 'automatic' visualization as that of a light ray bathing you from above.

As this occurs, you will see figures enter the great hall. Like the people of the city, they will be golden-haired and handsome, but their dress will be quite different to those outside. These figures will wear monk's robes in white, cowls thrown back to expose their faces. They will move perfectly silently, with serenity and order. They will take their places, in orderly rows, before the altar.

These figures will emerge from a number of entrances dimly seen beyond the colonnades of pillars. As they become evident – which should only happen *after* you experience the energizing sensation – move out calmly from between the twin pillars.

Walk again to the left of the altar (*your* left, that is, so that your total movement from the entrance in the west to the pillars and back takes you around the altar in a *clockwise* direction) and quietly take your place in the midst of the brethren. You will find that, soon after, one of them, the Hierophant, enters and after circling the great hall three times in ceremonial procession, takes his seat on the marble throne in the east.

Beyond this point, not even a tentative description is valid: your experiences will be uniquely your own.

Is there a case to be made for visualizing the sequence which follows the instruction 'and wait . . .'? Should you not, for instance, evoke a beam of light as you stand between the pillars?

Again, unfortunately, there is no direct answer. Your visualization will not be the real thing. The description was given here as a guide to what you may expect and a safeguard against the – unlikely – circumstances of a destructive contact.

As against that, visualization certainly helps build the forms that the Inner Plane entities activate. Bear in mind that you are still like the submarine commander using his periscope. The picture may, with practice, become clear, but it is never direct observation at this stage. Everything is seen and felt in the mirror of the Astral Light.

To a degree, therefore, the additional visualization may help. It was not included in the original instructions lest this part of the operation be thought of as a continuation of preparing the place of working. It is not. It is – or should be – the beginning of contact.

Inner Plane contact, as you will quickly discover when you establish it, carries a multitude of benefits. It is, for instance, a source of information – or perhaps 'wisdom' might be a better word. Much of the communication will be non-verbal in nature, insights, intuitions, convictions, which it will be up to you to catch and clothe in words to the best of your ability. Make a habit of taking notes immediately afterwards, each time you experiment with contact. Ideas and insights are easily lost unless this is done.

It is vitally important to remember that you have *NOT* been put in touch with some sort of super fortune-telling machine. Any attempt to treat Inner Plane contacts in this light will lead, at best, to their abrupt cessation.

A useful guideline for conduct is to assume you have had the good fortune to be introduced to a guru of remarkable insight – which, using this system, is exactly what has happened. Treat your contact with the respect due to such a sage and make sure, in advance, that the questions you may have are worthy and of relevance.

The establishment of Inner Plane contacts will usually make a very considerable difference to the outcome of any magical experiments you may undertake. Here again, it is impossible to formulate general rules, but there is usually a considerable stimulation *in accordance with the individual talents of the magician.* If, for instance, you have no flair for prophecy, the contact will not produce one. But if such a flair exists, you will find it coming quickly to the fore, increased in ease of operation and accuracy.

But as your evolution in the spiritual realities continues, a curious thing will happen. You will find it more and more difficult to perform certain operations of Low Magic. It's a curious paradox. The further you develop in the fascinating realms of magic, the less you can actually do. But there is a reason for it.

Magic and mysticism both lead, by vastly different tracks, in essentially the same direction. At the end of the road lies a state of contemplation – the reconciliation of the opposites, beyond all possibility of action. And before this state is reached, there arises an understanding of cosmic law and an acceptance of the karmic balance. It is as if you reached a stage in magic where further progress could only be purchased by the total acceptance of karma (what you sow, you reap). And not simply a theoretical acceptance either: the law must become a part of your being. In this state you could no more rock the boat than you can touch your right elbow with your right hand.

This does not, of course, mean you must cease to practise magic altogether, although even that will come about in the final stages when you grow beyond toys of any sort. What it does mean is that you will begin to concentrate on a *different type* of magic.

In the past, as you experimented with Low Magic, you used the forces to change your environment. To bring you a five-pound note, for instance, or discover a well so you could take a drink. But now the forces can be used increasingly in another direction. For as you grow in spiritual stature, you will realize that much more important than changing your environment is changing yourself.

It is this work on yourself that occultists refer to as the Magnum Opus. It was this operation the esoteric alchemists referred to as the discovery of the Philosopher's Stone, the mysterious element which would transmute base metals into finest gold.

## CHAPTER FOURTEEN

# GODFORMS

Every dramatist must be something of a wizard, just as every actor must be something of a medium. When a great play is written, its characters take on a life of their own. They become as real, for instance, as political figures you have never met; and often stick in the memory a great deal longer.

Of all dramatists, Shakespeare had the greatest talent for creating living characters. Hamlet and Prospero are personalities lacking only bodies to make them people. Falstaff was so imbued with vigour that he actually ran away from his creator.

A great actor does not, as many people imagine, interpret his part: he lets the part interpret him. By careful study and something curiously akin to meditation, he forms a link with the etherial character, then, medium-like, invites it to take him over. Such men as Olivier are not so much great actors as great puppets. They provide temporary bodies for Hamlet or Falstaff and these immortal creatures of another plane reach out and pull the strings.

The stage, more than any other art form, is magical in essence. The fact is probably quite widely recognized at an unconscious level, else why should we bother with theatres when we have the far vaster scope and technical perfection of the cinema? When a dramatist creates, he does something suspiciously like the magician's evocation of 'spirits from the vasty deep'. When an actor steps into a role, he does something suspiciously like the magician's assumption of a godform.

The assumption of a godform is, in a way, one of the most appealing operations in High Magic. Given the usual prerequisite of visualization ability, it requires no knack but work. And the bulk of the work, unlike so much of the grinding repetition of magical training, is interesting in itself.

There are a variety of reasons why you might wish to undertake the godform operation. You may, for instance, want to balance some aspect of your character. You may wish to investigate, at first hand as it were, the characteristics of the god concerned. Or you may wish to mediate the godforce for some specific purpose. Whatever your motive, the mechanics remain consistent.

The use of the godform (or, to be modern and scientific for a moment, the assumption of an archetype) is associated with ancient Egypt where it appears to have played a fairly major part in the magical life of the initiate priesthood. Among other references in *The Book of the Dead*, for instance, is one which reads, 'I have made myself a counterpart of Isis and her spirit hath made me strong.'

Because of this link, the forms assumed, even to the present day, tend to be Egyptian. Fortunately the pantheon is a self-contained and comprehensive system of magical images in its own right, which will amply repay the study necessary to use it nowadays.

The assumption of a godform is a potent method of invocation, the calling up of force to inward manifestation, as opposed to evocation which requires the force to manifest objectively.

To prepare the operation, you must first chose your god. There is no real reason why an archetypal godform from any pantheon may not be used, but the beginner would be well advised to stick to the Egyptian source. The use of Egyptian forms is traditional in magic: thus the operation becomes easier to perform since relevant channels are already half formed in the Astral Light.

Obviously your final choice of godform will depend entirely on the result you desire from the experiment. For the sake of illustration, let me assume that you have chosen the Egyptian Sun God, Ra.

Before attempting any magical operation, you must find out all you can about Ra. Egyptology has produced a prolific literature. Use it. Read the characteristics of Ra, the mythology of Ra, the descriptions of Ra. Never begrudge the time spent in this type of study: it is laying the foundations of a successful operation. Become an expert on Ra, so expert you could hold your own with any academic.

Pay particular attention to the god's appearance. That is, the appearance typically ascribed to him by artists. Take note of the characteristic poses in which he is depicted. *It is particularly important to know how the god was traditionally painted by the artists of ancient Egypt.* These men were, almost by definition, a degree closer to the source you are seeking.

Your library will almost certainly have books which will throw light on the subject. If not, ask the librarian to order some. Specially useful are the works of Wallis Budge, especially his *Gods of the Egyptians.*

When you study the traditional poses of the god, pay particular attention to gesture. These are seldom random and may be duplicated in your magical experiment with considerable benefit to the outcome.

Note too the implements traditionally associated with the god. Ra, for instance, traditionally carries an ibis wand in the left hand and an ankh (the Egyptian looped cross) in the right.

Only when you have steeped yourself in this sort of detailed knowledge, to a degree that it springs instantly to memory when needed, should you begin your actual experiments.

Magical exercises are best done in the morning, magical operations in the evening. Why this latter situation should pertain, I have not the least idea. But experience will show you get more results that way. It may be that the onset of darkness, which produces minor changes of consciousness in most people, is more conducive to magic which, in most of its aspects, requires a further change of consciousness in the operator.

So pick your evening for the assumption of the Ra godform. Or rather, pick your evenings, for you are unlikely to succeed at your very first attempt.

Your first step is to put your accumulated knowledge to use. Once again, you will be image-building, or, as the occultists say, creating stresses in the Astral Light.

Seat yourself in a comfortable position close to the traditional posture of the god. Then go through the relaxation process, combined with the 2/4 breathing sequence. If you can relax in the identical posture associated with the god, so much the better;

although this is not always possible. (Should the god's traditional posture be a standing one, as is the case, for instance, with Hathor, the Egyptian equivalent of Venus or Aphrodite, perform relaxation, breathing and initial visualization exercises in your usual meditation posture. Assume the stance of the god at the moment of assuming the godform.)

When you are totally relaxed, begin building up the vision. Again using the example of Ra, you should see the Sun God as a gigantic form standing before you, radiating light and heat. His form will be that with which you have already familiarized yourself through your studies.

Attempt to insert clarity and colour into your vision. Try to see the golden hue of the skin, the glowing nimbus around the head. Bring your other imaginary senses into play, so that you seem to feel the heat, seem to hear the lordly voice.

When you invoke a godform, you stand in the same relationship to the force behind it as a worshipper to his god. This is a point worth remembering, for the assumption of a godform cannot be a cold, scientific business. It involves deep emotions and a degree of commitment. Indeed, one of the most certain signs that your visualization has been successful is its ability to produce in you a feeling of awe.

The theory of the operation is straightforward enough. Ra as a person does not exist, and possibly never did. But the idea behind Ra is real enough. That is to say, the constellation of powers and characteristics which the Egyptians personified as Ra is real enough on another level of existence. (We are, in fact, back to the Inner Planes, but that is not important at the moment.)

The traditional pictures, postures and gestures of Ra are the forms, discovered through trial and error, through which the Ra-force can most easily manifest itself. These forms, through the activities of Ra's priesthood and devotees, gradually took on a semi-permanent existence in the Astral Light and effects, in ancient Egypt, followed fairly quickly and easily on any magical operation evoking or invoking Ra.

But as the Egyptian civilization degenerated, the astral forms faded into latency. There is a connection here with the occult theory of the artificial elemental. When a number of people concentrate with emotion on a single object, an artificial elemental is formed on the Astral Plane. The elemental persists only so long as it is fed by the emotion of the individuals.

Without worshippers, the gods can no longer exist on astral levels. But this does not mean the gods cease to exist altogether: the worshipper produces only the *form* of the god and not the *essence.* And the old forms are still best for manifestation.

Once you appreciate this, you will readily appreciate what you are doing in building up the vivid Ra image. You are, by an act of devoted concentration, producing a form through which the forces of Ra can manifest.

Provided you have built the form accurately, there will be little trouble in animation. Indeed, animation is something over which you have no control. Your job – at least your main job – is finished with the building of the form. The rest is up to Ra.

When the form has been established in the Astral Light to the greatest degree your talent allows, assume physically the traditional posture and gestures of the god. Then, by an act of imagination, have the astral godform coincide with your body. What you are, in fact, doing here is blending it with your own astral body, providing points of contact for the godforce to flow into you. As the form coincides (something which may take a little practice) invoke the god verbally.

Most authorities suggest you create your own invocation. The theory seems to be that this is nearer your true nature and consequently more likely to produce successful results. My own experience has been that traditional invocations work equally well, provided you choose one that genuinely appeals to you and do not use it simply because you feel you must.

A good (i.e. workable) invocation is like good poetry – it must affect the mind. If you find an invocation that inflames your imagination, use it. If you cannot find one, create one that does the job.

It may be of help to point out that there are two forms of workable invocation. The first, frequently used by beginners who do not realize there is another form, salutes the god as an exterior force and goes on to invite him to animate the prepared form. Thus:

'Hail to Thee, Ra. Eye of the Morning . . .'

The second form identifies with the god, as if animation of the assumed godform *had already* taken place. Thus:

'I have united myself with the divine Apes who sing at dawn and I am a divine Being among them . . .'

Whichever choice you make is largely a matter of taste, although identification does seem to have marginal advantages for the majority of operators.

Results of assuming a godform become evident the instant the operation is properly performed. The prime result is a staggering inflow of sheer energy, but as the practice continues, there is a gradual change in your own personality as it takes on more and more of the god's characteristics.

A danger here, seldom stressed, is that of one-sided development. Few of the old gods were fully-rounded, balanced personalities. But I assume that by the time you come to try High Magical experiments of this type, your development will be sufficient to ensure you realize dangers of this sort for yourself.

Since the assumption of a godform is a type of Inner Plane contact, the lengthy cleansing preparations outlined previously are relevant here. If you have already undergone the exercises in preparation for the Central Temple visions, there is no need to repeat them. But if not, do them before attempting the godform operation.

Complete the operation by separating the godform from your body, projecting it before you and gradually allowing it to fade away through an act of imagination. It is also no bad thing to complete proceedings with a ritual gesture, giving a clear demarcation line between your magical experiments and your life in the mundane world.

CHAPTER FIFTEEN

# CONJURATIONS

Ray leaned across and whispered, 'Have you gone into trance?'

I had not, but I had certainly sunk into reverie. We were at Mass and the sacrifice had been performed by one of the very few priests who seemed to know what he was doing. A Catholic, I assume, becomes accustomed to the Mass and thus, to a degree, hardened to it. For a Qabalist like myself, unfamiliarity made the ritual that much more striking.

The Mass is, of course, an excellent example of High Magic ceremonial, although often it goes unrecognized as such and outside the Liberal Catholic Church is all too frequently worked without power.

Like all magical operations, the Mass has an inner and outer aspect. Unfortunately Rome has either forgotten, or come to ignore, the inner aspect, with the result that too many priests gabble their way through the ritual.

But what a difference when the priest is a member of a contemplative Order, or has experienced the reality behind such visualization exercises as those of Saint Ignatius. In the hands of these men, the Mass suddenly comes to life and the congregation staggers off afterwards, emotionally uplifted, spiritually exalted and, one suspects, wondering what hit them.

During the Mass which had not, as Ray suspected, sent me into trance, I had been thinking of another magical operation I was privileged to watch a few years earlier. Unlike the Mass, it had not been open to the public.

The room was not particularly large, but it had apparently been reserved for magical operations so that a certain aura clung to it. It was part of a building owned, someone had assured me, by the Church. But this I doubt: the Irish love irony.

There was no carpet on the floor, but the boards had been scrubbed and polished. A double circle had been painted in lines about two inches broad, taking up most of the available space. To one side of the circle (I could not determine cardinal points in the room) was painted an equilateral triangle.

Inside the circle was a charcoal burner on a photographer's tripod. At each corner of the room was a large, lighted candle. While I regret to spoil a delightfully sinister story, none of these was black.

The magician was a minor disappointment too, as magicians usually are to those brought up on the dramatic works of Dennis Wheatley. He looked a little like a civil servant. That is, he conformed with my image of a civil servant: plump and balding, a man of about fifty. Doubtless civil servants look nothing like this, but, like everyone else, I preserve my images.

The magician – call him Carlos, for it points to the country where he was born – had been for many years a Spiritualist medium. But the philosophy of Spiritualism failed to satisfy him and he had moved on to more complex operations. He mixed magic with astrology and earned his living by trading in a variety of curious items.

Carlos had one assistant in his magical endeavours, an attractive young lady named Miranda, whom I had privately concluded he was attempting to seduce. It was Miranda who had secured my invitation to what would otherwise have been a very private ceremony. The portents being favourable, Carlos intended to attempt that rarest and most spectacular of all magical rites, evocation to visible appearance.

Evocation to visible appearance is something which has caught the public fancy. It is the operation fiction writers most often feature in their romances about magicians old and new. In fiction, the entities evoked are usually Satanic. How far this reflects the real-life situation I cannot say. I can only say I have never seen an infernal evocation, and indeed am aware of only a handful of men with the ability to perform evocation at all.

The basic pattern of an evocation can be easily described. The magician and his helpers crowd into the protective circle. From this fortress, the magician performs a rite designed to raise a spirit entity. If the rite is successful, the entity manifests within the confines of a triangle placed beyond the circle. If the operation stops there, it is a little more commonplace than the experiment I witnessed. The magician, unless endowed with psychic faculties, works with a clairvoyant. In a pattern which has remained unchanged since the days of John Dee and Edward Kelly, the magician questions the spirit through the clairvoyant.

Since this form of working will produce all the results you need, the infinitely more difficult evocation to visible appearance has been largely abandoned nowadays. The Order of the Golden Dawn used it as a grade test (the evoked spirit had to attain a consistency roughly equivalent to steam before the candidate passed). But since then only magicians like Carlos with attractive young assistants to impress would attempt it.

Unless some artificial adjunct is used, visible evocation can only be performed by a magician with certain physical characteristics. His bodily make-up must be such that he can manufacture that curious half-physical, half-etherial substance ectoplasm. Ectoplasm is produced in some mysterious manner from the gastric juices, and you can either spin it or you can't. The ability to produce it makes materialization mediums. But though Carlos was a medium, he did not specialize in materializations and was, in fact, unable to produce ectoplasm.

Without ectoplasm, the psychic entity must be presented with some other material suitable for moulding into a temporary body. This fact is part of the rationale behind bloody sacrifice (another part is the liberation of raw life-force). Blood is believed to give off a subtle evaporation which the spirit can use. But bloody sacrifice is a sickening business for an imaginative individual, and a magician is nothing if not imaginative. Consequently flowers, again believed to have a subtle evaporation, are often used; or, more frequently still and the case in the operation Carlos undertook, quantities of incense are burned.

Once the entity is called into the triangle, it uses the particles of incense smoke to build a body of sorts. The body is not very useful, but at least it is visible. Some race memory of the process is embodied in the Arabian Nights stories of the jinn who manifested in the smoke of a lamp.

Carlos was quite forthcoming about the details of his art. The circle, he said, would normally be fortified with Hebrew words of power, and symbols chalked on the floor between the double lines. The real circle, however, the important fortress, is on the Astral Plane and since the room was frequently used for evocation, this had been firmly established. The painted (physical) circle would form a guide to the outer limits of our protection, rather than a focus for the magician's mind, as was its more usual function.

How would Carlos perform the actual evocation? He intended to use a slightly modified version of a Hebrew ritual he had found effective in the past. He hoped I was a patient man, because it would probably take some time.

When it was time to begin, we left him alone for exactly twenty minutes. When we returned to the room (quietly, as he had instructed) he was wearing a long black robe, rather like a cassock, belted around the waist with a fringed white cord. He was kneeling inside the circle with his eyes closed, presumably checking up on the astral fortifications.

We entered the circle and I took up a position beside the incense burner, having agreed to work my passage by feeding incense and, more difficult, keeping the charcoal alight.

Carlos began the proceedings with a banishing ritual. I was forbidden to interrupt by asking questions, but by chance I happened to be familiar with it. It was the short, attractive Ritual of the Rose Cross (another Golden Dawn development) which does substantially the same job as the Pentagram Ritual, but leaves the atmosphere of a room somehow softer.

From that point on, I do not pretend to have any detailed knowledge of what went on. Carlos had said the ritual of evocation was Hebrew and I have no reason to doubt him. So far as I could judge, its form was similar to those medieval monstrosities such as are found in the Key of Solomon.

It took just over two and a half hours to reach a climax. By that time the room was filled with incense smoke, billowing in lung-choking profusion from the burner. Occasionally the lunatic fringe of the magical fraternity will add drugs to the incense in order to expand the consciousness of participants in ritual. No drugs were added here, but it is doubtful if they would have made much difference. The physical effect of two and a half hours in a small, darkened, smoke-filled room must be quite considerable.

Carlos, for all his civil service looks, had a good voice and he spoke the ritual well. The phrases had a rolling, sonorous quality which, I imagine, must tend towards the production of hypnotic effects when maintained over a sustained period.

Another factor in the situation was tension. We expected something to happen and for two and a half hours allowed our nerves to strain in a situation that was not exactly ideal for cold logical analysis.

Freedom of movement was relatively restricted. The room was small and our field of operation within the circle smaller still.

All these factors must have a cumulative effect, which is why I must end the story on a note of bathos. I am not sure if the evocation was brought to a successful conclusion or not.

It was an elemental evocation. That is to say, the force being called up was neither divine nor infernal, but neutral. At the climax of the ritual I stared with tear-filled eyes towards the triangle, half hidden in the fog of billowing smoke.

Was there a shape there? One moment my answer was yes; the next I was sure it was no. The smoke seemed to form a slimly-built, narrow faced man . . . then the illusion vanished – if it was an illusion.

I still do not know. But one thing is sure: the elemental conjured up by Carlos would never have earned him his grade in the Golden Dawn. It was just not solid enough.

An unusual reality, or imagination? If you read the works of Israel Regardie, and particularly his *Middle Pillar*, you will find an interesting theory put forward. It is a theory which attempts to reconcile two apparently diverse systems, Freudian psychology and magic.

Regardie argues, as I have done, that magic represents an archaic system of psychology. But at the time he put the theory forward, he, and nearly everyone else, was a lot more newfangled with Freudian ideas than might be the case today.

Freud's theories are so much a part of the intellectual establishment that it is difficult to appreciate how *avant-garde,* how revolutionary they appeared even thirty years ago.

Regardie saw, as others have noticed since, certain distinct similarities in the magical and psychiatric traditions. He suspected that, allowing for a different terminology, the two might be describing the same things.

Evocation, Regardie suggested, was a process parallel to psychoanalysis. He saw the magical operation as a means of dredging up unconscious complexes and presenting them, in the form of projected personifications, to the conscious.

If Regardie is right, then there is no doubt that the Carlos elemental was an hallucination in a very real sense of the world. The only real question remaining would be why I was seeing Carlos's hallucinations.

But Regardie is more a magician than an analyst. He would maintain that the mind is a much stranger place than Freud ever dreamed. Perhaps a complex can clothe itself with particles of incense smoke.

Or perhaps the whole thing is not merely an empty astral form (imagination/hallucination) after all. Perhaps the driving force lies deeper than the astral – in those Inner Planes on the other side of the mind.

## CHAPTER SIXTEEN

# CEREMONIAL MAGIC

I cannot evoke to visible appearance. My stomach has enough problems without asking it to produce ectoplasm and it seems to me much easier to use a good clairvoyant when information from spirit entities is required. But I do know a little about ceremonial magic which may be worth passing on.

The first thing I know is that magical ceremonial has the earmarks of a dying art. It is easy for the spiritually minded to forget mundane considerations. But forgotten or not, mundane considerations have a habit of making themselves felt, regardless. One of the most mundane considerations about magical ceremonial is that it costs money to mount.

According to tradition, the magician must make the tools of his trade himself. One old source I came across suggested that the magician's sword begins with his digging up iron ore. In modern practice, nothing of the sort happens. The apprentice will normally buy his materials and modify them.

Books take time to appear in print and prices seem to rise a little every day. So any detailed costing I might give now is almost certain to be out of date by the time you read it. Consequently I will content myself with listing a few of the items needed for ceremonial and allowing you to make up your own price list.

You will need a robe. The least elaborate may be purchased from a church supplier.

You will need a ring. Buy one if you must. Make one for preference. But making a ring requires materials and some lessons in the art of the silversmith.

You will need a room. Unless you have the space available at home, rent one.

You will need ritual furnishings (altar, pillars etc.). These are highly specialist items. Possibly you have the talent to manufacture them yourself. If not, they will have to be specially made and will almost certainly account for a major portion of your budget.

You will need a chalice. But a modified brandy glass will do, so this need not cost too much.

You will need a sword. Unless you have an iron lode in your back garden, hunt in antique shops. Congratulate yourself when you find a sword suitable. Wince when you hear the price.

You will need a dagger. Back to the antique shops again. If you are lucky, it will not be so costly.

You will need incense. The type of incense you use will vary in accordance with the particular magical operation. You will quickly learn that world supplies of raw materials for certain incenses are running out. The result has been a steep climb in prices for a number of years now.

Aleister Crowley, who was left a fortune by his father, recommended that equipment necessary for the art should be purchased without haggling, since the end return would more than outweigh the capital expenditure. But Crowley ended his life in Hastings, living largely on occasional donations from his followers.

As ceremonial grows more and more costly, it becomes increasingly the prerogative of groups. And even these are few enough and difficult to find.

Once an art form – and magical ceremonial is an art form – begins to contract in this way, a decreasing spiral comes into operation. You are faced with the law of diminishing returns. The craftsmen grow fewer. With fewer craftsmen, there are fewer teachers for the apprentices. So the apprentices themselves grow fewer. And this eventually leads to the further reduction of craftsmen.

What's to be done about it? I have long since lost my vision of utopian solutions. The chances are nothing can be done about it and nothing will be done about it. The great ceremonials, the ponderous rituals of initiation, evocation, thanksgiving and invisibility, will find less and less adherents until the pendulum swings in the other direction and ceremonial once again comes into its own as a branch of the magical arts.

In the final chapter of this book, you will find instructions for a magical operation almost as spectacular, but considerably safer, than evocation to visible appearance.

It is a frivolity and I have included it purely to satisfy an artist's promptings to conclude his work with a grand climax.

The operation is ceremonial in construction, so, dying art or not, you had better know something about the mechanics of a ritual working.

All magic, as you are now aware, works from the inside out. That is to say, magic is a mental science and the physical operations, spectacular though they may be, are nothing more than stimulants for mental processes.

The greatest single tool your mind uses is the symbol. You speak – and think – in word symbols. Your visualizations are picture symbols of reality. (So are pictures in a book, even the much more stylized diagrams in this one. You understand them because your mind is attuned to the use of symbols.)

If your mind uses symbols, it might almost be true to say that certain symbols can use your mind. Some configurations have an appeal that amounts to fascination and cannot be explained by logic. The cross, for instance, is one of them. It was used as a religious symbol for centuries before Christ. Why? Because the cross, as a symbol, has some deep-rooted, largely automatic effect on the human mind. Which is another way of saying nobody quite knows why.

Symbols can be visual, verbal, olfactory, tactile, graphic, simple or complex. One of the most complex symbols is a well constructed occult ceremonial.

To witness, or better still take part in a magical ceremonial is to have the senses assaulted from all directions. Many of the rituals embody an archetypal drama (death and rebirth is a favourite for initiation rituals) which can have a striking effect on the unconscious mind.

The circumstances enhance this effect. Even the most agnostic has some residue of tension about taking part in a magical ceremony. The lights are low, the candles flicker eerily. The mind is receptive . . . as the compilers of the ritual intended it should be.

All this is, of course, the ritual working from the outside inwards. But the reverse process is also under way.

Part of the inner working of many rituals is the process discussed in the last chapter, the assumption of godforms. Ritual participants mediate the spiritual forces and potent energies arising from the old gods, the angels and archangels and, in some cases, the elemental rulers. These energies, pouring through the participants, form, so to speak, a pool of power which is then directed by the ritual itself in order to further the work in hand.

No workable ritual can be constructed without considerable psychological knowledge. The great rituals of antiquity are, in the main, archetypally based, with the result that they can scarcely fail to produce some effect.

But there are other rituals, almost equally potent, which require a certain psychological training for their results. If the ancient rituals would please a Jungian psychologist, these latter appear to have been constructed expressly to delight behaviourists. The mechanics of behaviourism (association, conditioning, auto-hypnosis) are harnessed to the ceremonial cart, with results striking in proportion to the effort expanded in the preparation.

My personal familiarity with this form of ritual is largely based on Qabalistic work. An example drawn from this source will illustrate the mechanics. Through working on the Tree of Life, a Qabalist learns to associate many apparently diverse items. He would, for instance, associate the Moon, the colour purple, the mandrake plant, the perfume jasmine, the number nine and the Egyptian god Shu. All these associations, and many, many more, fall within the sphere of Yesod.

Assume for a moment that a Qabalist wished to construct a ritual which would put him in touch with the lunar (Yesod) forces. He would begin by establishing an environment in which as many items as possible drew his mind back to the central Yesod theme. He might, for instance, drape his entire temple in curtains of purple. He could place nine mandrakes on the altar. His incense would, of course, be jasmine. He might, like Carlos, engage the help of an attractive young assistant, for Yesod has distinct sexual associations. He could begin his ceremony with a reading of the relevant Yetziratic Text, 'The Ninth Path is called the Pure Intelligence because it purifies the Emanations. It proves and corrects the designing of their representations, and disposes the unity with which they are designed, without diminution or division . . . '

All this turns the Qabalist's mind in the direction of Yesod. And here the result of months, years, or even dozens of years of meditation becomes evident. The Qabalist's continual meditations form certain unconscious channels for the Yesod forces, and these are stimulated into activity by the ritual. Elaborate and impressive though the ceremonial may be, the channel is always the same – the mind (and on occasion the body) of the operator.

CHAPTER SEVENTEEN

# OPTICS AND ILLUSIONS

Most things reflect light. You and I sense these reflected rays in the process we call seeing. When there is no light source present, we see nothing. This we experience as a sort of three dimensional blackness.

Under certain lighting conditions, glass is invisible. Instead of reflecting, light rays pass completely through it. And under certain lighting conditions, mirrors are invisible. This is because a mirror reflects light too well. Our attention is caught by the image. Our eyes are dazzled by the reflection. We see something, but not the mirror itself.

You will note that the experience of looking at something invisible, such as properly positioned glass, is vastly different from not being able to see it while light is totally absent.

From the point of view of physics, invisibility occurs in practice when light rays pass completely through an object. It occurs in theory when light rays are bent around an object and straightened out on the far side. (This remains theoretical. As far as I know, light rays cannot be bent in this manner.) Invisibility does not occur when all light is absorbed by an object. You may not be able to see the object, but you will certainly be able to see there is something badly wrong.

All this is schoolboy optics at a very naive level. It is worth recapitulation since most people think of invisibility, when they bother to think of it at all, in terms of the behaviour of light rays.

But there is a second form of invisibility which has nothing whatsoever to do with light rays. Once it is explained, people usually find it a lot easier to accept than the pseudo-explanations of Wellsian science fiction.

If you walked into a room which contained, let's say, Miss Bardot in a bikini, you might be forgiven if you failed to notice me sitting quietly in a corner. There are people who seem fated not to be noticed whether Miss Bardot is present or not. Their personalities, or lack of them, ensure that they are perpetually overlooked. They are nature's nonentities, the colourless people who make little impression. You will, I am sure, agree you have met them – although you may well find difficulty in recalling their faces. As your eye slides over these nonentities at a party, they are, to all intents and purposes, invisible to you. Their presence does not register. They blend with their background. They have the invisibility, not of glass, but of the chameleon.

Any competent hypnotist can show you this psychological trait pushed to extremes. A subject in deep trance can be told there is no one in the area of the room where you are sitting. When he looks, he will not see you. Should he attempt to sit in your chair, he will land on your knee with total bewilderment. When the spell is broken, he will apologise profusely, explaining that he *did not notice you.*

Here, perhaps, is a secret of invisibility worth examining. What makes one person notice another? Movement, for one thing. A moving object is easier to distinguish than a static one. Certain animals know this instinctively and freeze in moments of danger. A variety of predators know it too and impose a type of movement on the scene by bobbing their heads while hunting.

But if you wish to be overlooked, try sitting perfectly still. Positioning plays a part. Put crudely, you are less likely to be seen in a corner than in the middle of the room. More subtly, the lighting and decor of a room will tend to produce a focus of attention. Move out of this area and you are less likely to be noticed.

These, and such obvious factors as whether or not you chatter, are physical aspects of the problem of why you are noticed. But they do not seem to be *all* the aspects. One man sitting still in a corner will draw attention like a magnet. Another will be virtually invisible. The difference between the two appears to lie on the psychological level.

Some things are so commonplace that we never think about them. Yet it is really a remarkable thing that my attention will be instantly drawn towards another human being in a room even though he is (apparently) doing absolutely nothing to attract it.

Occultists, who accepted telepathy long before Rhine proved it in the laboratory, assume the reason why this happens is a contact between minds.

Not, of course, anything specific. But even if you cannot read thoughts, you may be perfectly aware of a stream of consciousness. The little man inside our skulls keeps up an incessant chatter. If I may use an exploded analogy, the transmitter is broadcasting garble and while your receiver picks up no detail, you are aware of the direction of the signal.

This sort of theory leads to a very specific line of approach to the whole interesting, if rather fruitless, problem of invisibility. Suppose you were able to shut off the garble; would this not, in theory, produce a situation in which you were less likely to be noticed? The answer is yes, but the problem of shutting off the garble is fairly acute. It seems the simplest thing in the world to stop thinking . . . until you try it. Yogis will frequently spend a lifetime practising just this one single trick.

The Oriental may be prepared to exercise such extraordinary feats of patience. The Westerner, having tried a few times and failed, tends to turn his attention on the possibility of a short cut.

If I make myself known to you in a darkened room by talking, my most obvious way to hide is to stop talking. But if I am cursed with an irresistible compulsion to keep on talking, my next best move is to surround myself with a soundproof screen. It is this form of thinking that lies at the root of the invisibility ritual given here.

The sequence is an abridged and modified version of a ceremonial used in the Golden Dawn. The full ritual is a massive affair and, from a practical viewpoint, probably reflects a Masonic love of ceremonial for its own sake. Those interested, however, should refer to Israel Regardie's major work *The Golden Dawn*, recently reissued in two volumes and available in Britain through its distributors, The Aquarian Press.

# CHAPTER EIGHTEEN

## RITUAL INVISIBILITY

First prepare your place of working. You need space for ritual working and the more you skimp, the more difficult the working will be. Pick a reasonably sized room and clear it out completely. It goes without saying you should make sure you will not be disturbed.

Set up your altar in the centre of the room. A small table draped with a black cloth will do. The top of the altar is a working surface. Arrange to have it at a height that suits you.

To the east of the altar there should be the twin pillars – the black pillar on your left as you face east, the white, or silver pillar on your right. It is unlikely that you will be able to find and erect suitable pillars for the ritual, but if not, they should still be represented. You might, for instance, use two boxes, or even two discs painted the relevant colours. But be sure to visualize the pillars strongly; and always behave as if they were whole and entire.

For the surface of the altar, you will need a Calvary Cross and an equilateral triangle. Both may be cut from cardboard, and both should be painted red.

You will also need a goblet of water and a lamp. The lamp should be small enough to carry and of the type fuelled with oil or something similar.

Place the cross to the east on the altar, with the triangle to the west. The lamp stands in the south, the cup below the triangle in the west.

Although not strictly necessary for the performance of the ritual, it is as well to balance these elemental symbols by placing a rose (symbol of Air) to the east and bread and salt (symbol of Earth and the fruits thereof) to the north.

When you are ready to begin, perform the Banishing Ritual of the Pentagram. Make sure the ritual has worked (there is a curious but unmistakable sensation of emptiness when the astral atmosphere is cleansed) before continuing with the ritual. If in doubt, start again. The original ritual recommends using the Banishing Ritual of the Hexagram as well, but this seems unnecessary, *provided the Pentagram Ritual is carried out properly.*

Now, while standing at the altar, facing east, recite the following invocation.

'Ol Sonuf Vaorsag Goho Iad Balt, Lonsh Calz Vonpho. Sobra Z-ol Ror I Ta Nazps, od Graa Ta Malprg. Ds Hol-q Qaa Nothoa Zimz, Od Commah Ta Nobloh Zien. Soba Thil Gnonp Prge Aldi. Ds Vrbs Oboleh G Rsam. Casarm Ohorela Taba Pir Ds Zonrensg Cab Erm Iadnah. Pilah Farsm Znrza Adna Gono Iadpil. Ds Hom Od Toh. Soba Ipam Lu Ipamis. Ds Loholo Vep Zomd Poamal Od Bogpa Aai Ta Piape Piaomel Od Vaoan. Zacare Eca Od Zamran. Odo Cicle Qaa. Zorge Lap Zirdo Noco Mad. Hoath Iaida.

'Adgt Vpaah Zong Om Faaip Sald, Vi-i-vl, Sobam Ialprg Izazaz Pi Adph, Casarma Abramg Ta Talho Paracleda, Q Ta Lorslq Turbs Ooge Baltoh. Givi Chis Lusdi Orri, Od Micalp Chis Bia Ozongon. Lap Noan Trof Cors Ta Ge O Q Manin Iaidon. Torzu Gohe L. Zacar Eca Ca Noquod. Zamran Micalzo Od Ozazm Vrelp. Lap Zir Io-Iiad.'

Despite appearances, the words are far from gibberish. They form, in fact, a tiny part of one of the most potent magical systems yet discovered – the Enochian Calls.*

This system dates back to the days of Queen Elizabeth the First, when the astrologer/magus John Dee conducted a series of experiments in evocation with the clairvoyant, Edward Kelly. These experiments involved the evocation of certain angels into a crystal where Kelly apparently saw them. One of these angels dictated the Enochian Calls, letter by letter and backwards, lest the powers they commanded be called up accidentally.

Dee's original notebooks with the Calls are preserved in the British Museum (along with the crystal in which Kelly saw the angels) and scholars have since reluctantly decided the unlikely language contained its own grammar and syntax.

The Call above is an invocation. When you have completed it,

* For a guide to the pronunciation of Enochian, see *Appendix Three*.

hold still a moment and experience the force flow it controls. Then,

'In the name of Yeheshuah, Yehovashah, I invoke the power of the Recording Angel. I adjure thee, O Light invisible, intangible, wherein all thoughts and deeds of all men are written. I adjure thee by Thoth, Lord of Wisdom and Magic who is thy Lord and God. By all the symbols and words of power; by the light of my Godhead in thy midst. By Harpocrates, Lord of Silence and of Strength, the God of this mine Operation, that thou leave thine abodes and habitations, to concentrate about me, invisible, intangible, as a shroud of darkness, a formula of defence; that I may become invisible, so that seeing me men see not, nor understand the thing that they behold.'

Go to the east, kneel and meditate on the Sephirah Binah on the Tree of Life. (Should your Qabalistic training be limited, it is as well to read as much about the sphere in advance as possible. Some such work as Dion Fortune's *The Mystical Qabalah* is recommended.)

Return to the altar and, visualizing Binah as the Supernal Mother, address her.

'Lady of Darkness who dwellest in the Night to which no man can approach, wherein is Mystery and Depth unthinkable and awful silence. I beseech Thee in thy name Shekinah and Aimah Elohim, to grant thine aid unto the highest aspirations of my Soul, and clothe me about with thine ineffable mystery. I implore Thee to grant onto me the presence of Thy Archangel Tzaphqiel (pronounced Zaf-key-el) the great Prince of spiritual initiation through suffering and of spiritual strife against evil, to formulate about me a shroud of concealment. O ye strong and mighty ones of the sphere of Shabbathai, ye Aralim, I conjure ye by the mighty name of YHVH Elohim (Yod-hey-vav-he El-o-eem) the divine ruler of Binah and by the name of Tzaphqiel, your Archangel. Aid me with your power, in your office to place a veil between me and all things belonging to the outer and material world. Clothe me with a veil woven from that silent darkness which surrounds your abode of eternal rest in the sphere of Shabbathai.'

Now comes what is essentially a stilling of the mind through an invocation of Hoor-po-krat-ist, Lord of the Silence. The name should be vibrated in the Kether position, then circulated through the aura by means of the Middle Pillar exercise given earlier. Then,

'Hoor-po-krat-ist, Thou Lord of the Silence. Hoor-po-krat-ist, Lord of the Sacred Lotus. O Thou Hoor-po-krat-ist, Thou that standest in victory on the heads of the infernal dwellers of the waters wherefrom all things are created. Thee, thee I invoke, by the name of Eheieh and the power of Agla.'

Meditate for a moment on the incoming force represented by the God, then, visualizing Hoor-po-krat-ist strongly, continue.

'Therefore I say unto Thee, bring me unto thine abode in the Silence Unutterable, all-wisdom, all-light, all-power. Bring me to thee, that I may be defended in this work of art. Bring me to thine abode of everlasting silence, that I may awake to the glory of my godhead, that I may go invisible, so that every spirit created, and every soul of man and beast and everything of sight and sense and every spell and scourge of God, may see me not, nor understand.

'And now, in the name of Elohim, let there be unto the void a restriction. Be ye opened, ye everlasting doors, that the King of Glory and of Silence and of Night may come in.

'Thus do I formulate a barrier without mine astral form that it may be unto me a wall and as a fortress and as a sure defence. And I now declare that it is so formulated, to be a basis and receptacle for the Shroud of Darkness, the Egg of Blue with which I shall presently girdle myself.'

Now comes a second, shorter Enochian invocation.

'Ol Sonuf va-Orsagi Goho Iada Balata. Elexarpeh Comananu Tabitom. Zodakara, Eka Zodakare Od Zodameranu. Odo Kikle Qaa Piape Piamoel Od Vaoan.'

Then,

'And unto ye, O ye forces of the Spirit of Life whose dwelling is in the invisible, do I now address my will. In the great names of your ruling Angels Elexarph, Comananu, Tabitom, and by all the names and letters of the Holy Tablet of Union, by the mighty names of God, Eheieh, Agla, YHVH Elohim, and by the great Lord of Silence, Hoor-po-krat-ist, by your deep purple darkness and the brilliant light of the Crown above my head do I conjure thee. Collect yourselves about me, and clothe this my astral form with an egg of blue, a shroud of darkness. Gather yourselves, ye flakes of Astral Light, and shroud my form in your substantial night. Clothe me and hide me, but at my control. Darken men's eyes that they see me not. Gather at my word divine, for ye are the watchers and my soul is the shrine.'

Perform the Qabalistic Cross then visualize vividly the blue-black egg materializing around you. On no account rush this portion of the operation, for it is possibly the most important for results. Your entire attention should now be taken up with the idea of becoming invisible. Say,

'Let the Shroud of Concealment encircle me at a distance of eighteen inches from the physical body.

'Let the Egg be consecrated with fire and water . . . '

Do not proceed to consecration (which tends to stabilize the astral form) until you are completely satisfied with your formulation of the Egg. For the consecration place the lamp on your right and the water on your left and repeat,

'O Auramo-oth and Thaum-Aesh-Neith, ye Goddesses of the Scales of the Balance, I invoke and beseech you that the vapours of the magical water and this consecrating fire be as a basis on the material plane for the formation of the Shroud of Art.'

Again visualize the Egg as strongly as possible. Go to the east of the altar, facing initially west, turn three times on your own axis, then say,

'In the name of the Lord of the Universe and by the power of my Augoeides and by the aspiration of thine own higher soul. O shroud of darkness and of mystery, I conjure Thee that thou encirclest me, so that I may become invisible. So that seeing me, men may see me not, neither understand. But that they may not see the thing that they see, and comprehend not the thing that they behold. So mote it be!'

Circle the temple, clockwise, once, then go to the south and, facing the altar, visualize twin pillars of fire and cloud. Visualize the shroud hanging between them. Move to the west and say,

'Invisible, I cannot pass by the Gate of the Invisible, save by virtue of the Name of Darkness.'

Visualize the Egg enveloping you again and affirm.

'Darkness is my Name, and Concealment. I am the Great One Invisible of the Paths of the Shades. I am without fear, though veiled in darkness, for within me, though unseen, is the magic of the Light Divine.'

Go to the north and perform the same visualization you did in the south. Say,

'Invisible, I cannot pass by the Gate of the Invisible, save by virtue of the Name of Light.'

Visualize the Egg clearly. Then,

'I am Light shrouded in Darkness. I am the wielder of the forces of the Balance.'

In your imagination, see the darkness of the Egg growing even more intense. Return to your former position to the west of the altar, and say,

'O thou divine Egg of the creative darkness of spirit, formulate thou about me. I command thee by the name of Yeheshuah. Come onto me, Shroud of Darkness and of night. I conjure ye, O particles of spiritual darkness that ye enfold me as an unseen guard and as a shroud of utter silence and of mystery. Egg of divine darkness, shroud of concealment, long hast thou dwelt concealed. Quit the Light, that thou mayest conceal me before men.'

Again see the shroud formulating around you.

'I receive thee as a covering and a guard. Khabs Am Pekht. Konx Om Pax. Light in Extension. Before all magical manifestation cometh the knowledge of the hidden light.'

Stand between the pillars of the temple, facing west and allow the Egg to formulate around you, gradually causing your physical form to fade from sight. Walk three times around the temple clockwise, then say from the east:

'Thus have I formulated unto myself this shroud of Darkness and Mystery as a concealment and a guard.

'Supernal Splendour which shinest in the sphere of Binah, YHVH Elohim, Aima, Shekinah, Lady of Darkness and of Mystery, Thou High Priestess of the Concealed Silver Star, Divine Light that rulest in thine own deep darkness, come unto me and dwell within my heart, that I also may have power and control, even I, over this shroud of darkness and of Mystery. And now I conjure thee, O shroud of Darkness and of Mystery, that thou conceal me from the eyes of all men, from all things of sight and sense, in this my present purpose, which is to remain invisible for the space of – hour(s) and to receive therein the holy mysteries of the Lord of Silence enthroned upon his Lotus, Hoor-po-krat-ist.'

And so the ceremonial concludes. Since cars require brakes and poisons antidotes, the reversal ceremony to regain visibility is given in Appendix Two.

# APPENDIX ONE
## The Qabalistic Colour Scales

| | *Atziluth* | *Briah* | *Yetzirah* | *Assiah* |
|---|---|---|---|---|
| Kether | Brilliance | White brilliance | White brilliance | White, flecked gold |
| Chokmah | Pure soft blue | Grey | Mother of pearl | White, flecked red blue and yellow |
| Binah | Crimson | Black | Dark brown | Grey flecked pink |
| Chesed | Deep violet | Blue | Deep purple | Deep azure flecked yellow |
| Geburah | Orange | Scarlet | Bright scarlet | Red flecked black |
| Tiphareth | Clear rose pink | Golden yellow | Rich salmon | Gold amber |
| Netzach | Amber | Emerald | Yellow-green | Olive flecked gold |
| Hod | Violet purple | Orange | Russet | Yellow brown flecked white |
| Yesod | Indigo | Violet | Dark purple | Citrine flecked azure |
| Malkuth | Yellow | Citrine, olive russet and black | Citrine, olive russet and black flecked gold | Black rayed yellow |

# APPENDIX TWO

## Regaining Visibility

Return to your temple and perform the Qabalistic Cross, visualizing vividly. Then say,

'In the name of YHVH Elohim, I invoke thee who art clothed with the sun, who standest upon the moon, and art crowned with the crown of twelve stars. Aima Elohim Shekinah, who art Darkness illuminated by the Light divine, send me thine Archangel Tzaphkiel and thy legions of Aralim, the mighty Angels of the sphere of Shabbathai, that I may disintegrate and scatter this shroud of darkness and of mystery for its work is ended for the hour.

'I conjure thee, O shroud of darkness and of mystery which has well served my purpose that thou now depart unto thine ancient ways. But be ye, whether by a word or will, or by this great invocation of thy powers, ready to come quickly and forcibly to my behest, again to shroud me from the eyes of men. And now I say unto ye, Depart ye in peace, with the blessing of God the vast and shrouded one, and be ye very ready to come when ye are called.'

Visualize the shroud disintegrating, then close with the Pentagram Ritual forcefully performed.

# APPENDIX THREE

## A Guide to the Pronunciation of the Enochian Calls

The invocation given in Chapter Eighteen is a small part of one of the most difficult and complex, yet altogether fascinating, magical systems ever devised.

As a means of producing practical results, the Enochian System has a considerable reputation among occultists. Yet because of its inherent difficulties, it is probably true to say that those currently attempting its practice are few in number. The Enochian Calls, their application and philosophy, formed part of the old Golden Dawn system, integrated – at least to some degree – into the vast structure of Qabalistic doctrines taught in that organization. Today, I am only aware of one Fraternity working the Enochian System to any great extent – the Order of the Cubic Stone, operating out of the English Midlands.

Although the origin of the Calls can be traced back only as far as Dee and Kelly with any degree of certainty, the Enochian language itself is held to be very much older. Analysis of certain key words suggests it predates Sanscrit. Tradition has it that the language is 'angelic', used in the distant days when communication with the higher spheres was rather more common that it is now. Another school of thought holds it was the spoken language of lost Atlantis.

The invocation forming part of the Rite of Invisibility comprises the first two Enochian Calls. Since the original revelation was dictated letter by letter rather than spoken, there is no 'authorized' pronunciation guide.

Pronunciation does, however, present considerable difficulties, especially in those words where consonant follows consonant without vowel intervention. Fortunately, we have the help of considerable practical research by Golden Dawn members on this point. From their findings, it seems the best practical spoken form of the language is developed by taking each letter separately in those words where lack of vowels makes this necessary. Most of the consonants are pronounced as they are in English with the following exceptions.

Z becomes Zod, with a long 'o'. A becomes Ah, rather than Ay. P becomes Peh, rather than Pee. B becomes Beh. D becomes Deh. T becomes Teh. V becomes Veh.

In sounding vowels, I is pronounced as 'ee', while E is invariably short, that is, pronounced Eh, as in 'bed'.

As an example, a difficult word such as 'Znrza' in the Call, would be pronounced *Zod-en-ar-zod-ah.* 'Ds' is pronounced *Deh-ess.* 'Eca' is pronounced *Eh-ka.* 'Vpaah' is pronounced *Veh-peh-ah-ah-heh.*

Once these principles are grasped and, more important, once the 'swing' and rhythm of the invocation is picked up, pronunciation difficulties tend to fade quite quickly.

The invocation may also be performed in English, although the effect will not be so pronounced. The English translation of the relevant Calls is given below. Even if you intend to employ the original Enochian, study of the English is recommended: it is always as well, in a magical operation, to understand what you are saying.

'I reign over you saith the God of Justice, in power exalted above the Firmament of Wrath: in Whose hands the Sun is as a sword and the Moon as a thorough-thrusting fire: Who measureth your garments in the midst of my vestures and trussed you together as the palms of my hands: Whose seat I garnished with the fire of gathering: Who beautified your garments with admiration: to Whom I made a law to govern the Holy Ones: Who delivered you a rod with the Ark of Knowledge. Moreover ye lifted up your voices and sware obedience and faith to Him that liveth and triumpheth: Whose beginning is not nor end cannot be: Which shineth as a flame in the midst of your palace and reigneth amongst you as the balance of righteousness and truth. Move therefore and show yourselves: open the mysteries of your Creation. Be friendly unto me for I am the servant of the same your God, the true worshipper of the Highest.

'Can the wings of the winds understand your voices of wonder, O You the Second of the First, Whom the burning flames have framed within the depth of my jaws: whom I have prepared as cups for a wedding or as the flowers in their beauty for the chamber of the righteous. Stronger are your feet than the barren stone and mightier are your voices than the manifold winds. For ye are become a building such as is not save in the Mind of the All-Powerful. Arise, saith the First. Move therefore unto thy servants. Show yourselves in power and make me a strong seer of things, for I am of Him that liveth forever.'

find in Spiritualism) but a mass of deception, mutual and self, as people without much drama in their lives got together in a conspiracy to produce some.

In this atmosphere oddities occasionally occurred. The human mind is a curious thing and the group mind is even odder. In the dim light with emotions roused, strange things happened. A stirring subconscious might stretch out telekinetic tendrils to produce a poltergeist or two. An hysterical woman might, quite unconsciously, steal information from another mind.

Such things happen daily among Spiritualists. They have nothing to do with post mortem communication (although confusion between the two is rife amongst the faithful) but may someday prove a mine of interest to the parapsychologists. They are the platinum beneath the E.P.N.S.

Very many years later, still searching for the miraculous, I found myself alone in London. It was a quiet end of the city, an avenue with trees where you could actually forget you stood upon a plain of concrete that stretched for miles without a break whichever way you turned.

My taxi-driver had looked up at the houses, sucked in breath and opined that the nobs lived here. But he was only trying out applied psychology in the hope of a bigger tip. Anyone with half an eye could see the district was in decline. The nobs had once lived here certainly, but not any more. Those who remained were strictly members of the stranded gentry.

I walked through a little garden overgrown with shrubs. The greenery was London green, as if soot had managed to discolour the living plants. I rang the bell.

It was as if I had been swept back through the years. The woman who opened the door would have dropped into that phoney seance without creating a ripple on the surface. She was, by physical type, one of the fat poor. But she was completely silent, which was totally out of character for the type.

I went to a little ante-room where I prepared myself with meditation for some fifteen or twenty minutes. Then I was escorted down a flight of stairs to a very different sort of seance. The room was a Lodge Room, constructed and prepared by ritualists. It was furnished with, among other things, the traditional altar and pillars. Lodge officers, mediating archetypal figures, stood, or sat, at the cardinal points. There was incense and candlelight.

There was also, it occurs to me now, the utter professionalism – no other word can describe it – of a group that knows what it is doing.

The room had been prepared by ritual, almost certainly a variation of the Pentagram Ritual given earlier. It had, I presume, been used time and again for evocation. The effect of that room was staggering.

If you have ever walked any distance on a frosty winter's day before pushing open a door into a centrally-heated building, you will know what I mean by a wall of air. There was a wall of air at the doorway of the Lodge Room. But its essence was not heat but something else, something that could be sensed perfectly (and, it seemed, at a physical level) by the nerve endings beneath the skin of the face. Houses have 'atmosphere', a welcoming feeling or a rejection, an aura of warmth or chill. This was atmosphere solidified, an atmosphere that literally 'hits you in the face'.

There were no fireworks in the working that followed, no trances or weird shadows in the incense smoke – just results and an atmosphere pregnant with power.

The essential difference between these two groups was that the second I described had formed a link with the Inner Planes and was drawing power from the other side of the collective mind. The first group had power too, for it produced occasional phenomena. But it was power drawn only from the subconscious and to that extent was phoney where the operation of High Magic is concerned.

Inner Plane contacts are most often made within a group setting. The trick is easier that way. But links may be forged by individuals, if they go about it the right way.

There are, in fact, a number of methods. They produce different kinds of contact, although all originate in essentially the same area. It is as if you had three friends in New York. One

# Other recommended books...

## YOUR PSYCHIC POWERS

**And How to Develop Them**

**Hereward Carrington Ph.D.** The *only* detailed instruction manual of its kind for developing trance-mediumship! This amazing book, written by a dedicated psychical researcher, was based on notes he wrote for circulation amongst members of New York psychical societies. Introduces the whole range of psychic manifestations, including the human aura, telepathy, clairvoyance, crystal gazing, automatic writing, obsession and insanity, hypnotism and mesmerism, astral projection, spirit- and thought-photography and materialization. Guidance is also given in distinguishing between true and false phenomena. Dr. Carrington maintained: **'. . . we are all more or less mediumistic or psychic, and need only to cultivate our powers in order to develop them, and bring them to maturity.'**

## THE MAGIC OF THE RUNES

**THEIR ORIGINS AND OCCULT POWER**

**Michael Howard.** Fascinating introduction to the history, development and magical use of the runic alphabet, an ancient form of writing shrouded in mystery. Includes detailed instructions for casting the runes for purposes of divination. The runes were used by initiates of occult traditions to pass on magical information. The unusual angular strokes of the runes is probably due to the fact that they were originally hewn into stone, thus precluding curves and rounded letters *Other contents:* Secret of the shamans; Odin the man; Regalia of the rune masters; Origins of Ogham script; Druidic tree alphabet.

## THE TECHNIQUES OF ASTRAL PROJECTION

**OUT-OF-THE-BODY EXPERIENCES**

**Robert Crookall B.Sc.(Psychology).** Almost anyone who hears of cases involving astral projection regards them as mere dreams. But people who actually experience this phenomenon are convinced of its reality, as revealed in the fascinating documentation presented in this book. Moreover, people who have never heard of each other, much less compared notes, make identical statements about their astral experiences, and these occurrences correspond with cases that have been carefully investigated. *Includes:* 'Blackout' caused by the release; Discarnate 'hinderers' and 'helpers'; Range of astral travel.